Mrs Wordsmith®

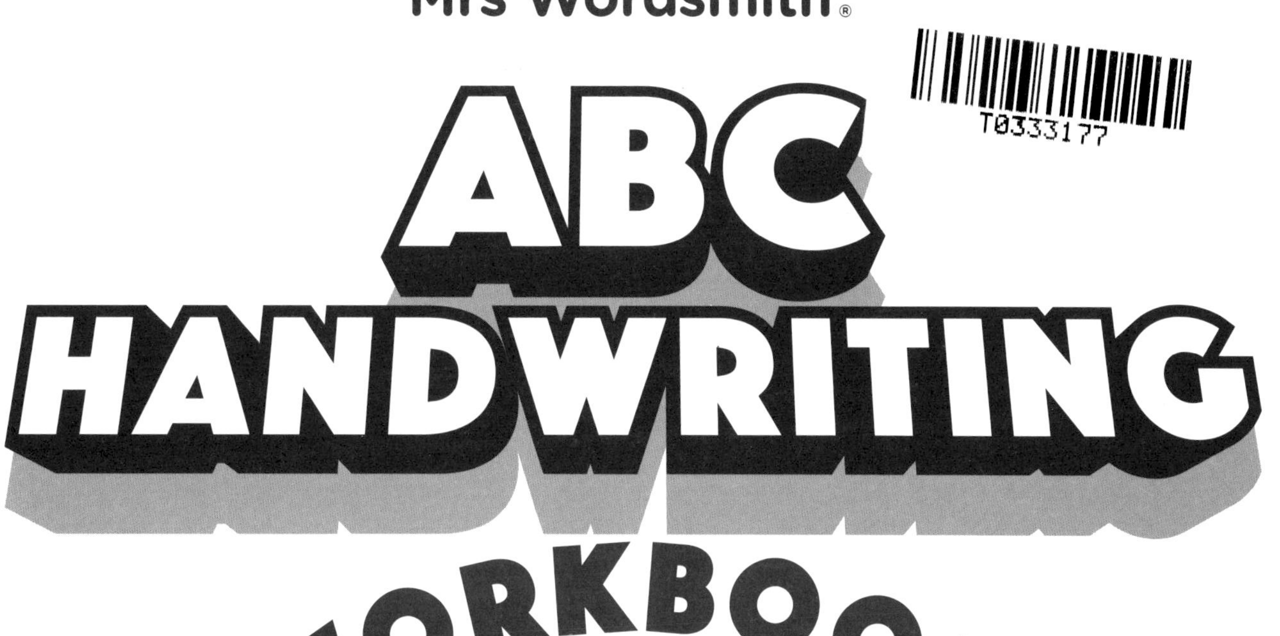

WORKBOOK

A Z

STORYBOOK WITH HANDWRITING PRACTICE

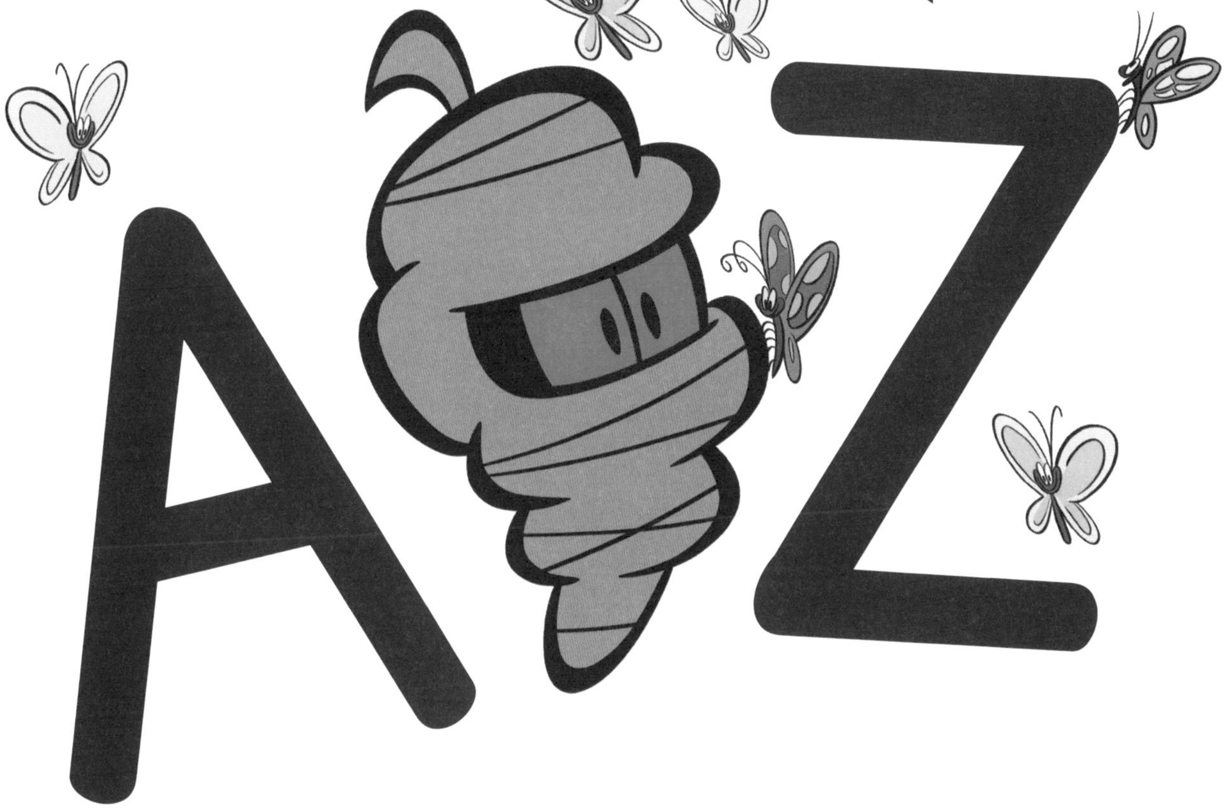

This book belongs to:

....

Mrs Wordsmith®

ABC HANDWRITING WORKBOOK

mrswordsmith.com

This story takes you through the whole alphabet. Practise writing each letter on the handwriting page and scan the QR code to hear the letter sound.

Help Bogart chomp his way from A to Z and face his greatest fear - being ordinary.

Scan the QR code with the camera on your smartphone or tablet. Some devices will require a QR scanner to do this. This can be downloaded free from your app store of choice. If you have any trouble, you can find more detailed instructions at mrswordsmith.com

Contents

Pooville was a very ordinary town filled with very ordinary flies.

The food in Pooville was always the same.

Poo for breakfast.
Poo for lunch.
Poo for dinner.

Bogart was not like the other baby flies. Bogart was different.

He was afraid that if all he ever ate was poo, he would grow up to be a common housefly.

He would be ordinary.

Bogart had dreams. Big dreams.
Dreams of escaping Pooville.
Dreams of becoming...

...a butterfly!

If he could eat something besides poo...

If he could chomp, chew, and crunch his way through the alphabet...

He could make his dreams come true.

He would chomp until he was transformed into a beautiful butterfly.

He would chomp from A to Z!

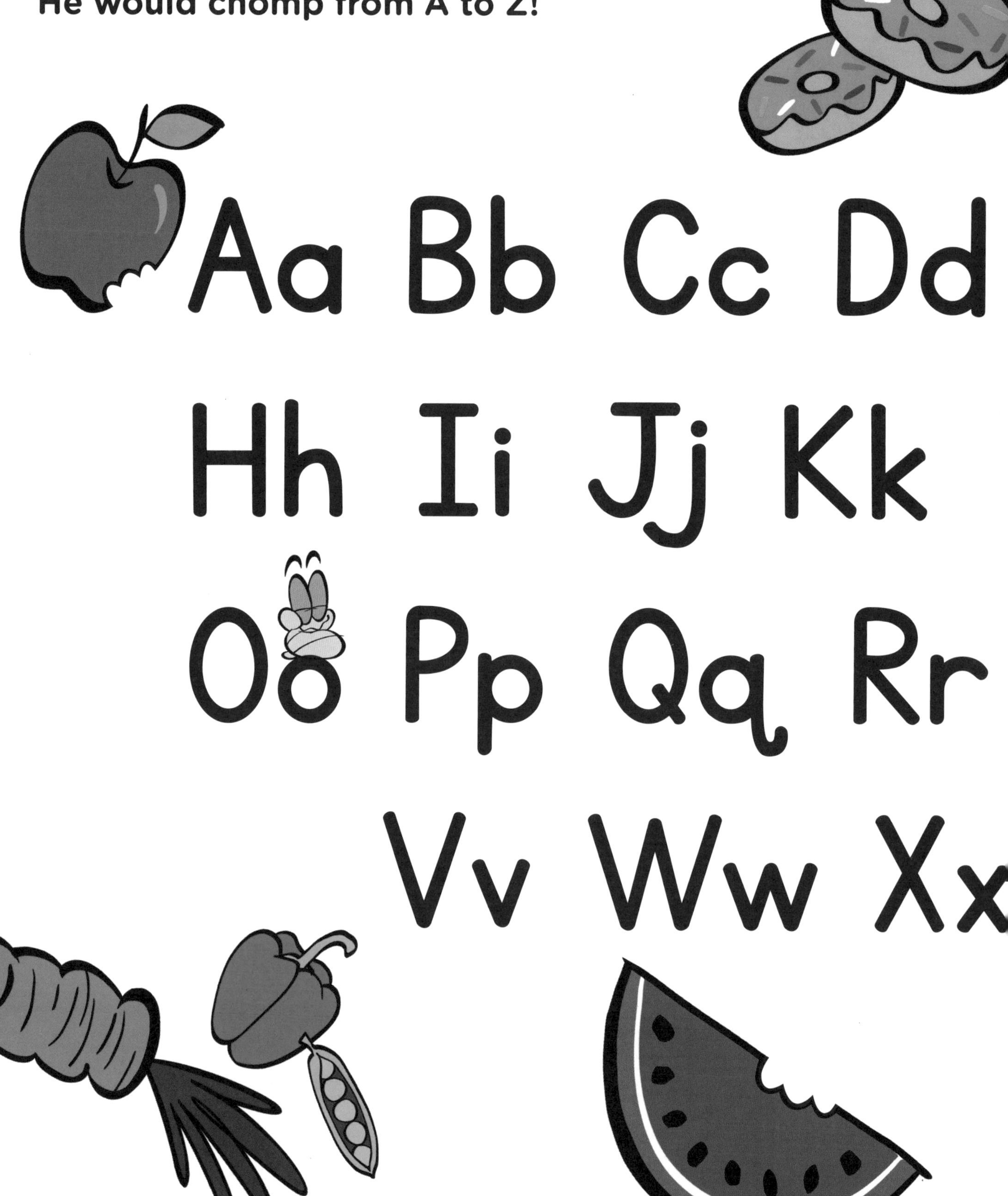

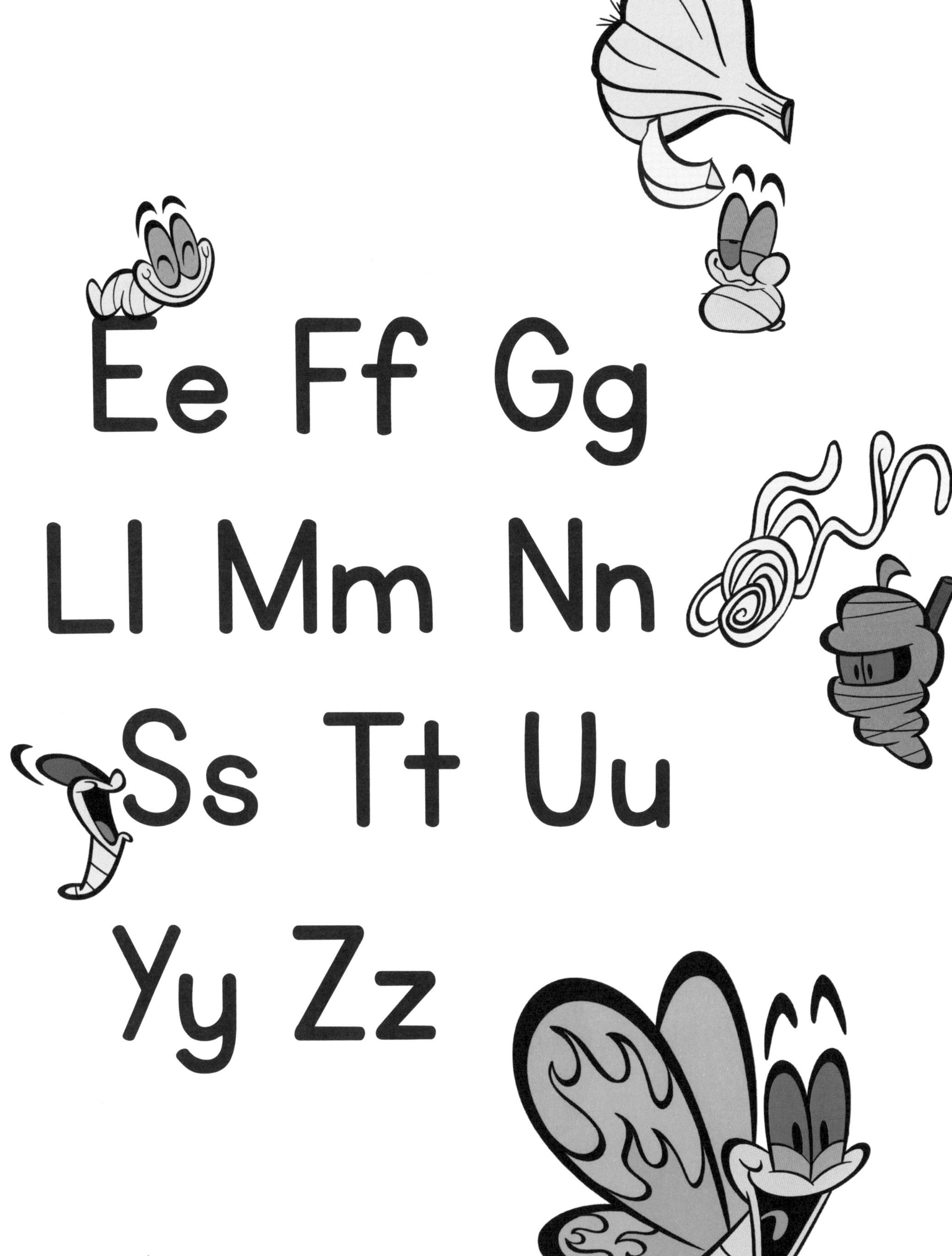
Ee Ff Gg
Ll Mm Nn
Ss Tt Uu
Yy Zz

Bogart's foodie **adventure** began with the letter **A**.

He wanted to eat everything healthy that started with the letter **A**.

I will chomp apples and avocados.

1. Follow the arrows to write the letter.

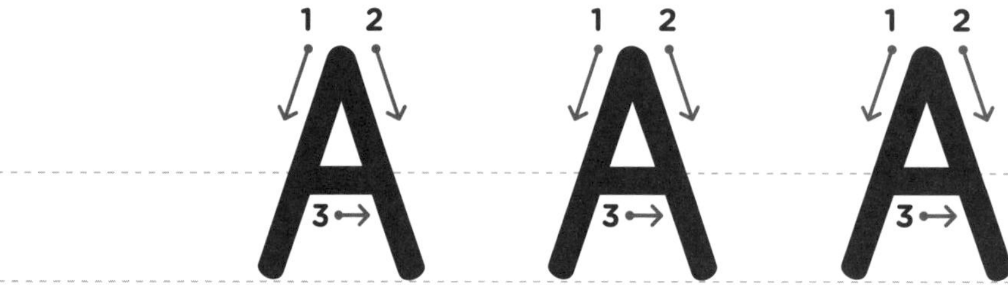

2. Trace the letter.

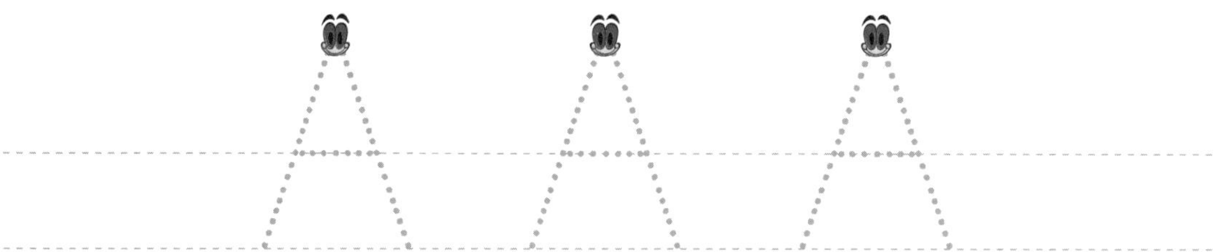

3. Now try writing it! Start with Bogart's emoji.

Play the sound
with the QR!

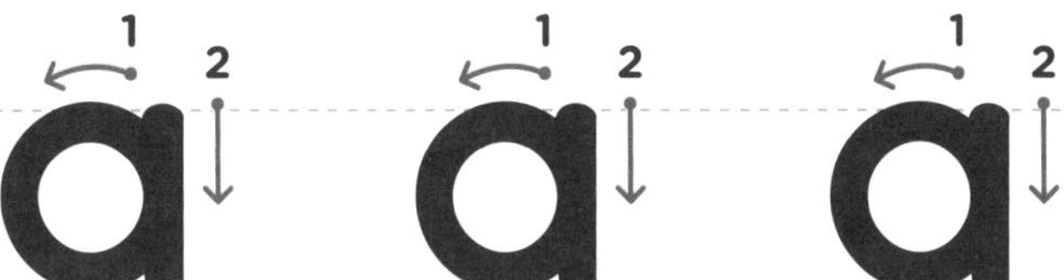
1
2
a
1
2
a
1
2
a

Next, the letter **B** for **Bogart**!

I will chomp **bread**, **bagels**, **burritos**, and **burgers**.

Bogart was only just **beginning**.

Bb

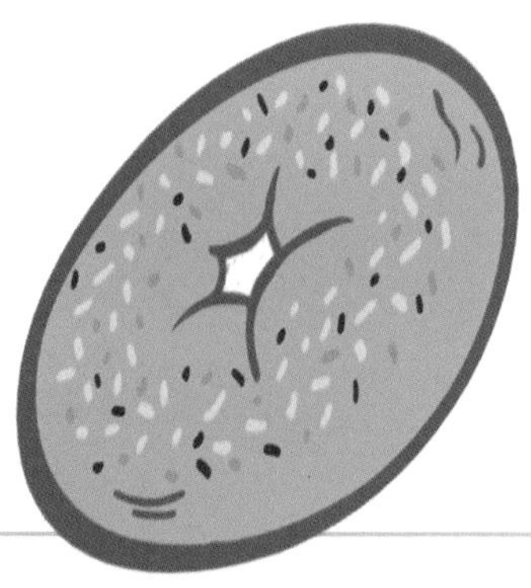

1. Follow the arrows to write the letter.

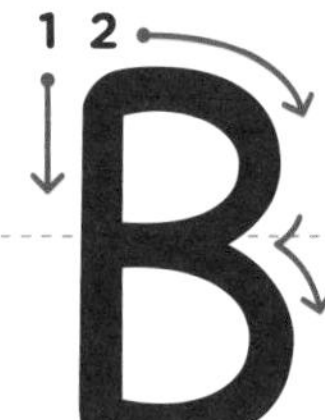
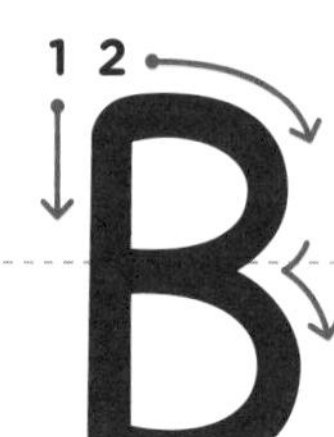
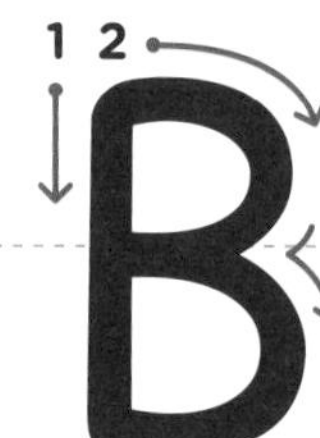

2. Trace the letter.

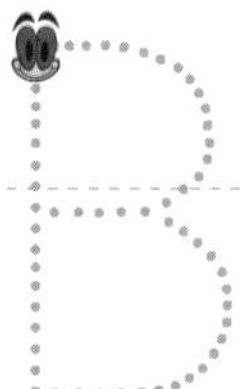
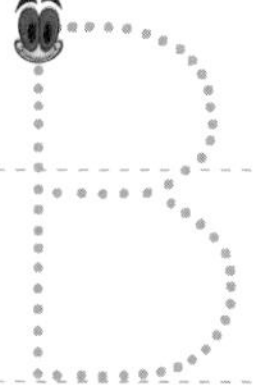
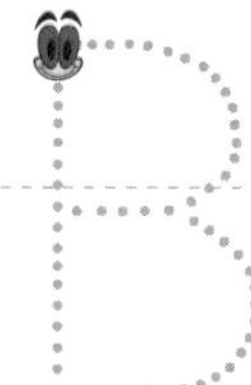

3. Now try writing it! Start with Bogart's emoji.

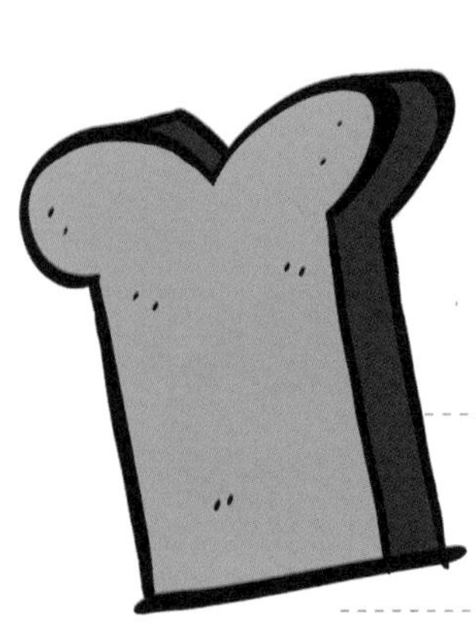

1 2 b 1 2 b 1 2 b

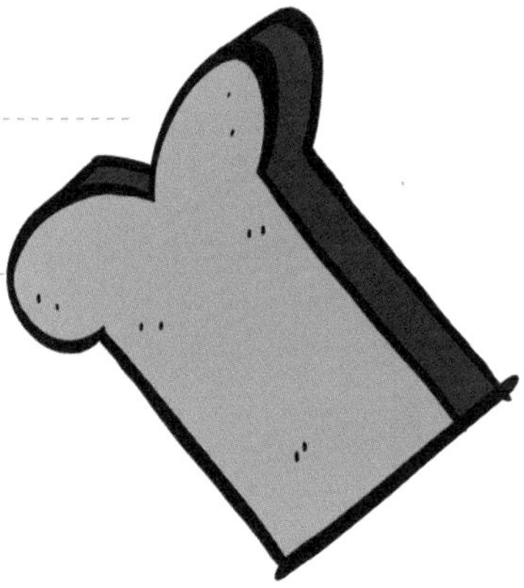

b b b

b b b

At the letter **C**, Bogart **craved** something sweet.

I will **chomp** **cakes** and **cookies**.

Then, he had
his first sugar rush.

Cc

1. Follow the arrows to write the letter.

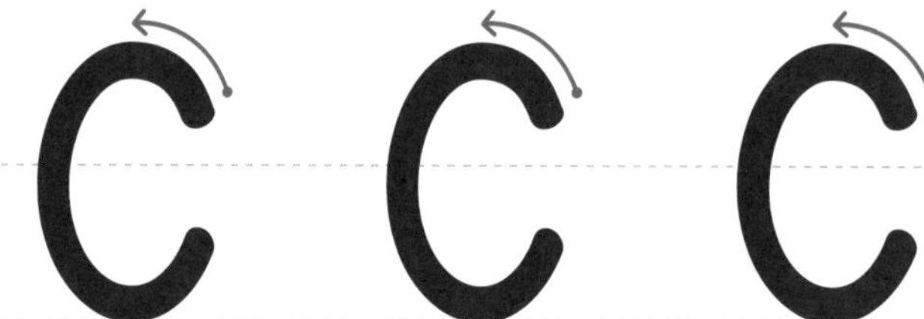

2. Trace the letter.

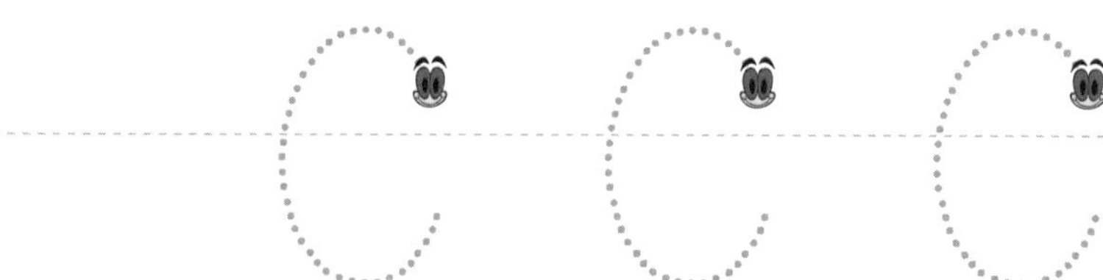

3. Now try writing it! Start with Bogart's emoji.

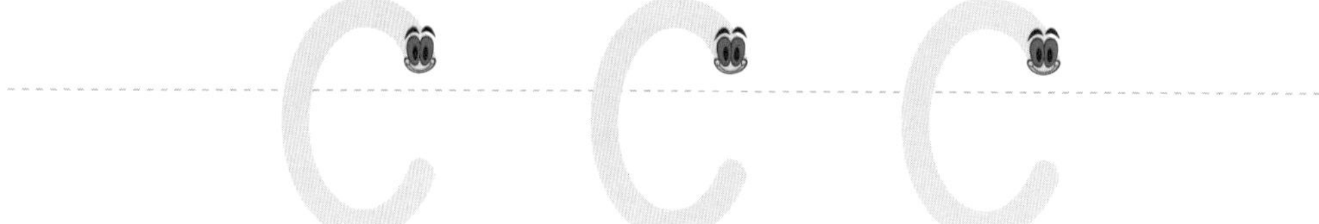

Play the sound
with the QR!

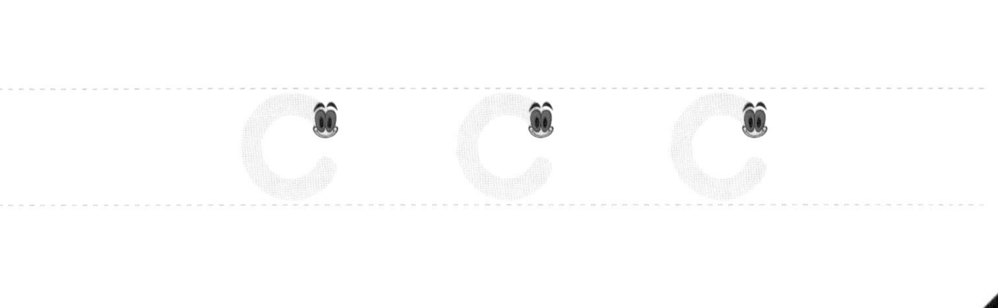

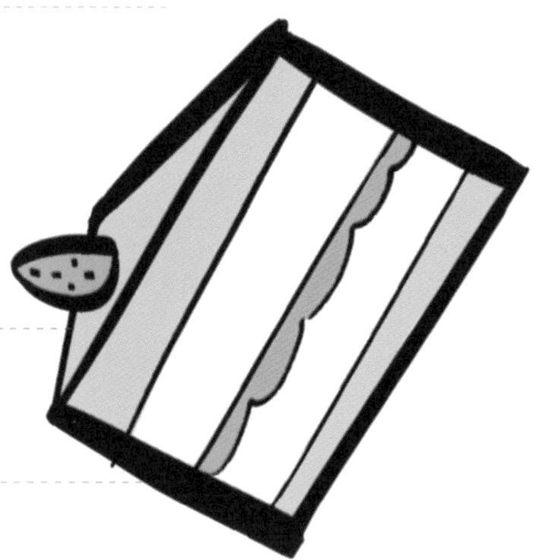

Bogart was **desperate** for more sugar.

I will chomp
dozens of delicious doughnuts!

Dd

1. Follow the arrows to write the letter.

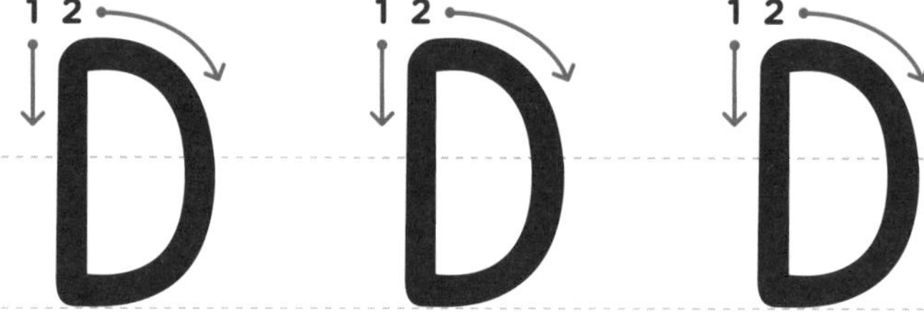

2. Trace the letter.

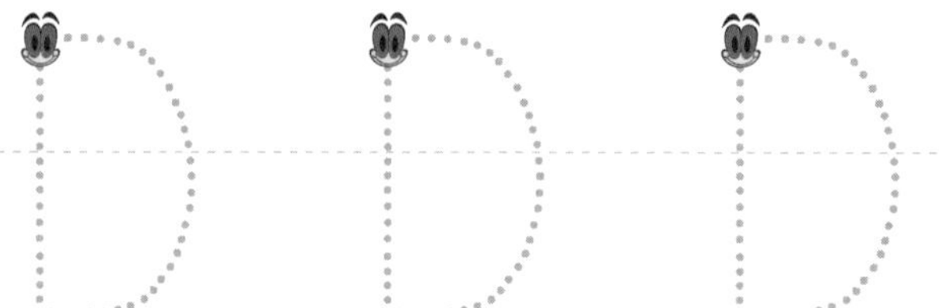

3. Now try writing it! Start with Bogart's emoji.

Play the sound
with the QR!

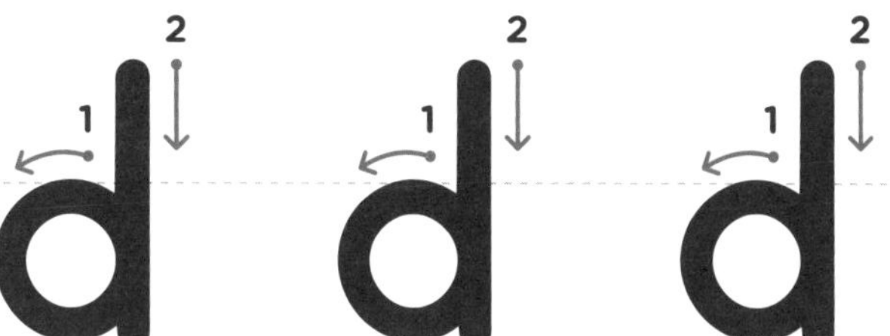
1
2
1
2
1
2

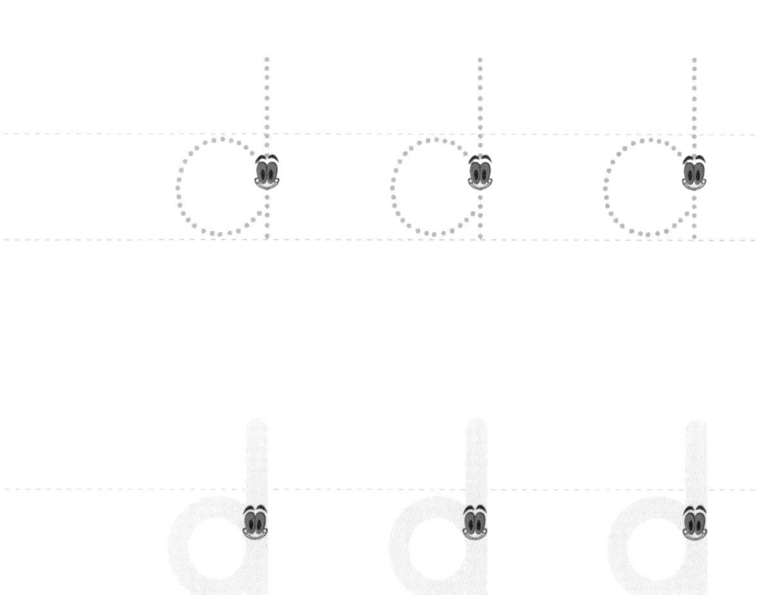

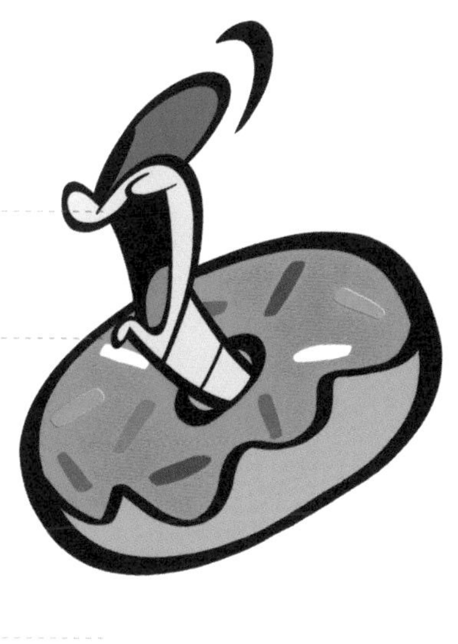

At the letter **E**,
Bogart kept chomping.

I will chomp eggs.

How do you chomp your **eggs** in the morning? Boiled, fried, scrambled, or poached?

Ee

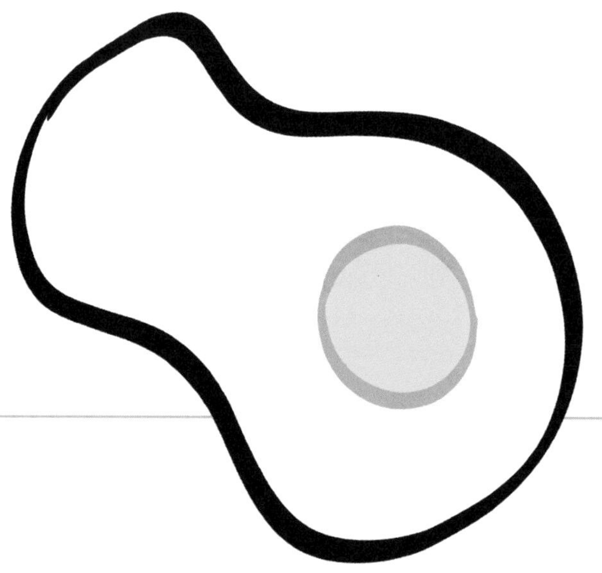

1. Follow the arrows to write the letter.

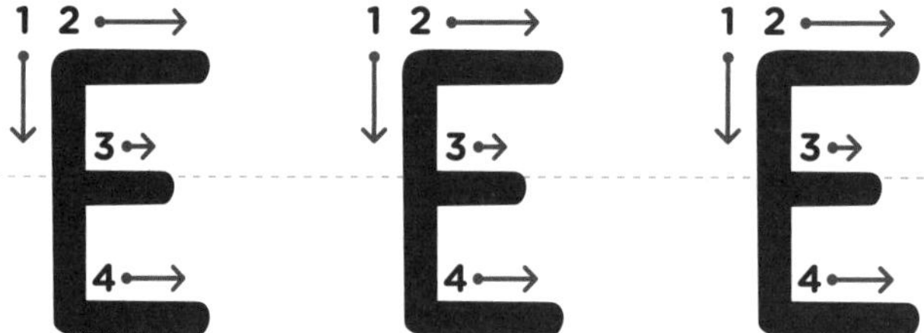

2. Trace the letter.

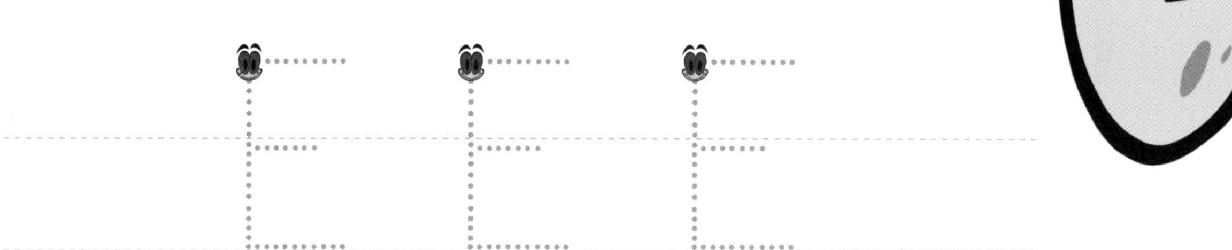

3. Now try writing it! Start with Bogart's emoji.

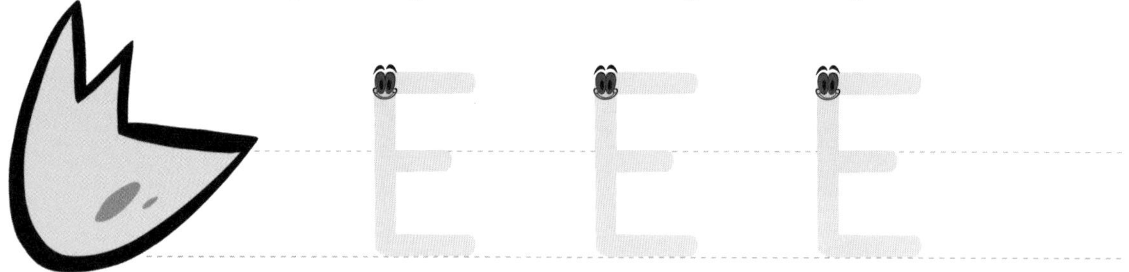

Play the sound with the QR!

e e e

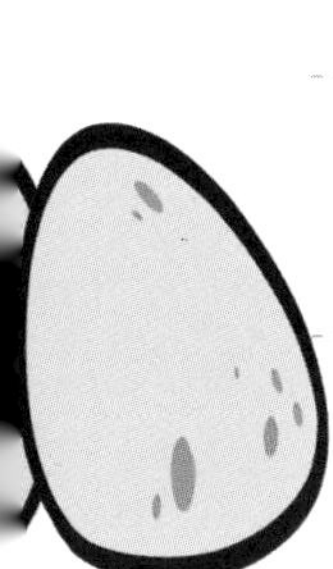

If Bogart ate the letter **F**, would he **float** or would he **flounder**?

f

Ff

1. Follow the arrows to write the letter.

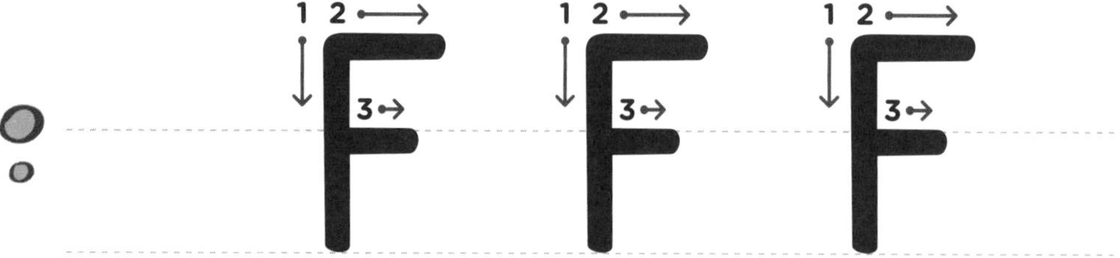

2. Trace the letter.

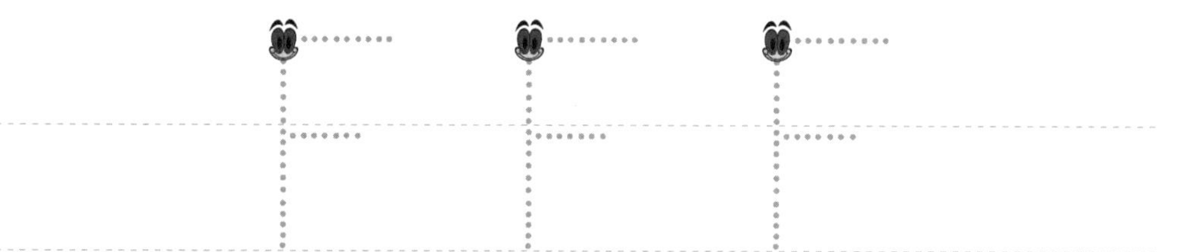

3. Now try writing it! Start with Bogart's emoji.

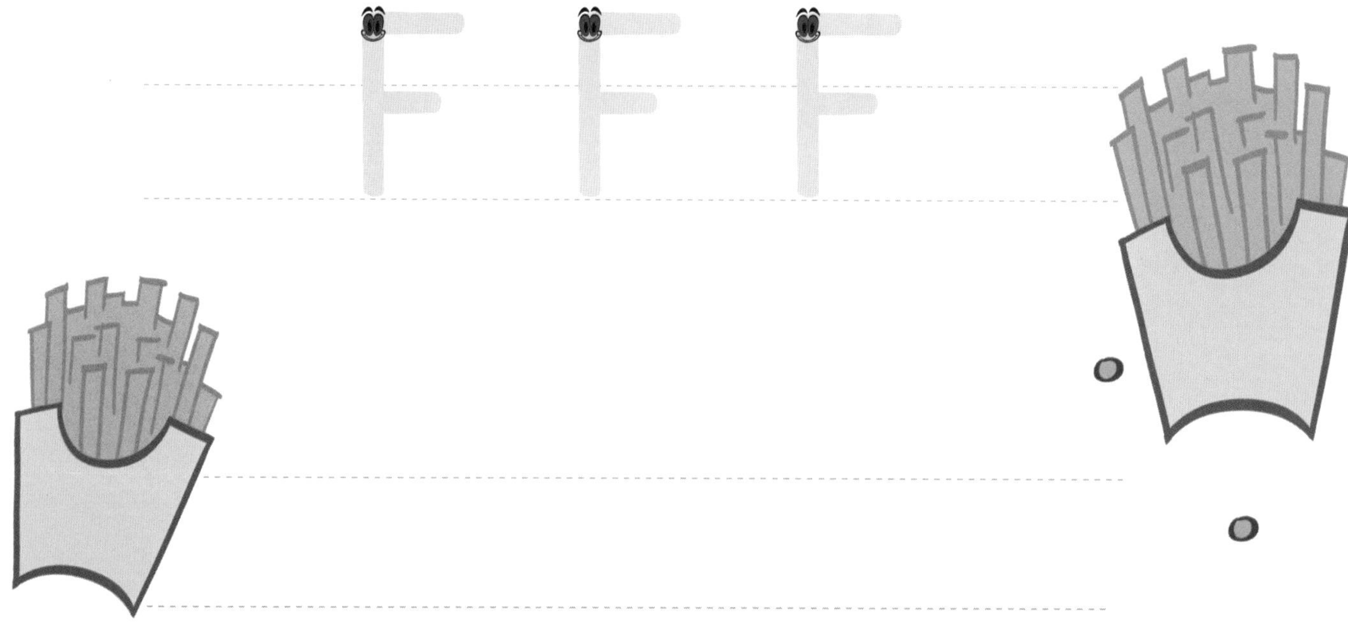

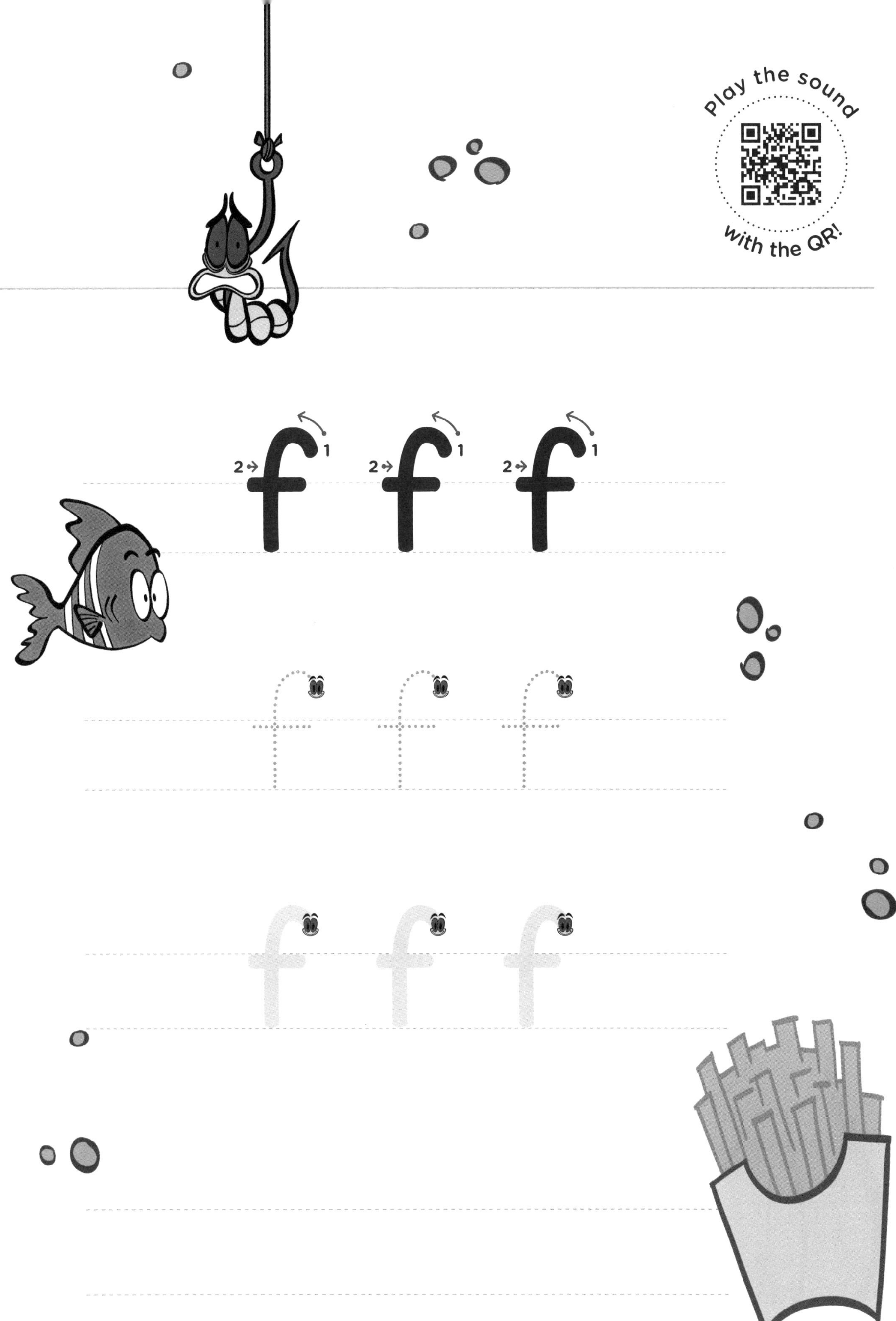
Play the sound with the QR!
2 1 f f f

When Bogart arrived
at the letter **G**, he paused
to think...

He could chomp **grapes**
or **green** beans.

But instead, he winked...

I will chomp
garlic and my breath will stink!

Gg

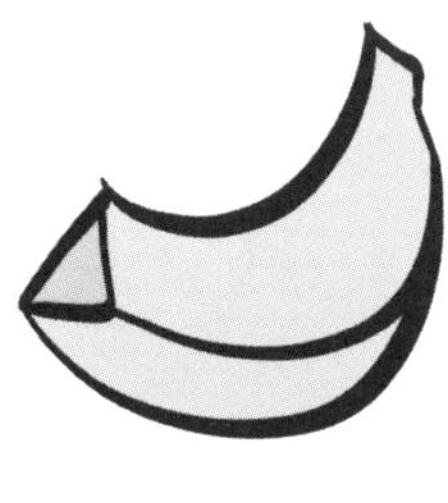

1. Follow the arrows to write the letter.

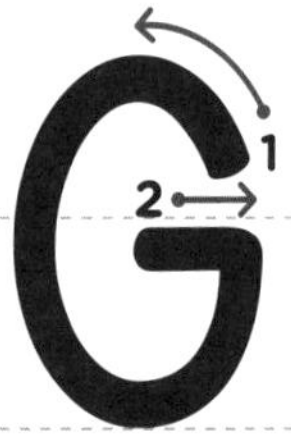

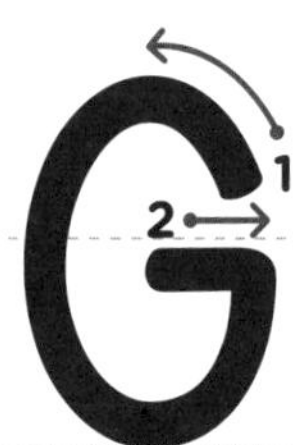

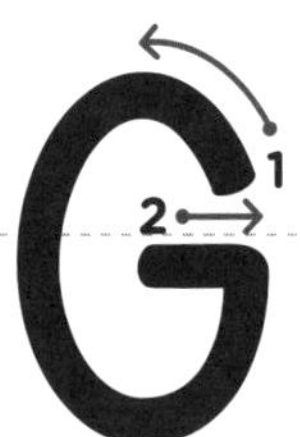

2. Trace the letter.

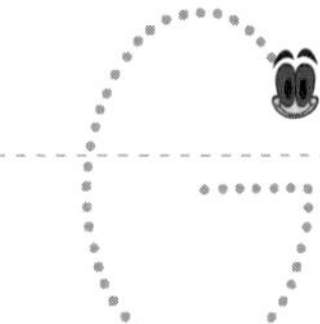

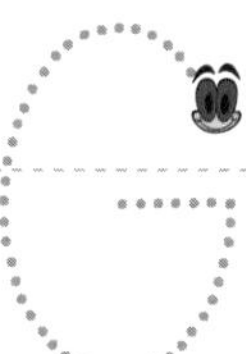

3. Now try writing it! Start with Bogart's emoji.

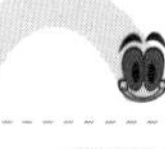

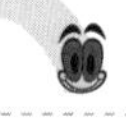

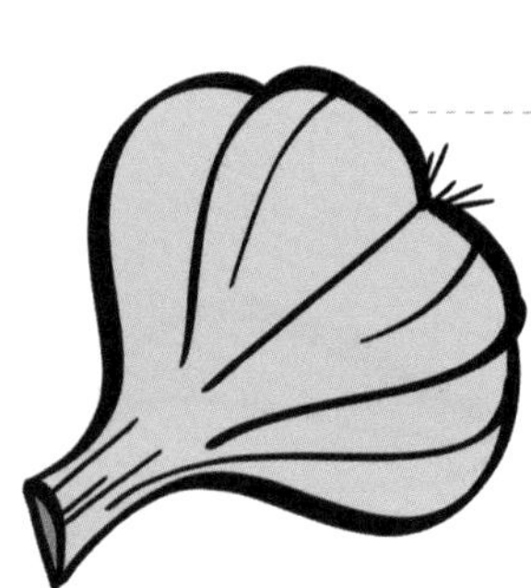

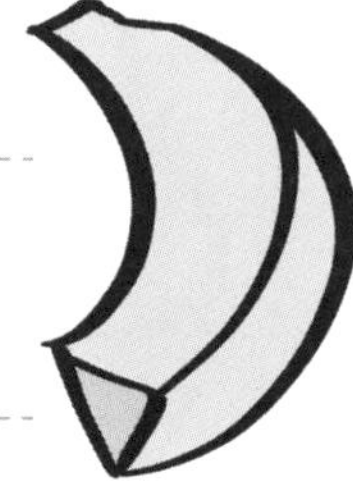

g g g

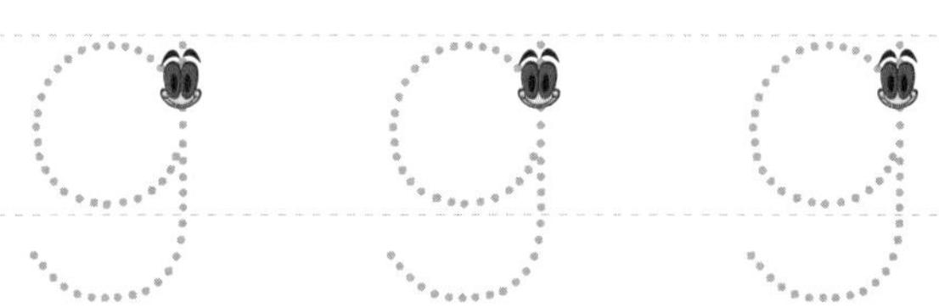

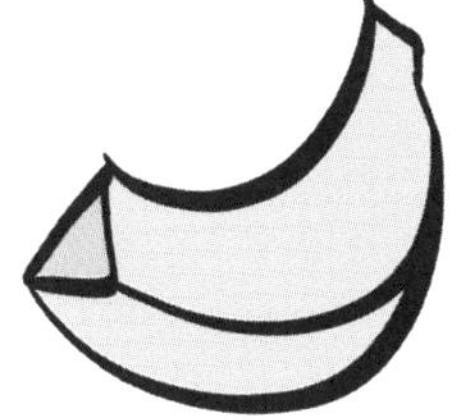

At the letter **H**, Bogart wanted to fly **high** like a butterfly!

He didn’t think **ham**, **hummus**, or **hazelnuts** would shoot him into the sky...

I will chomp
a hovering helicopter.
Hh

Hh

1. Follow the arrows to write the letter.

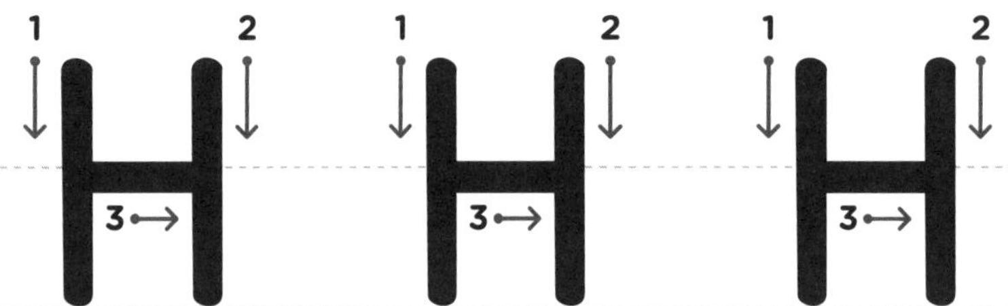

2. Trace the letter.

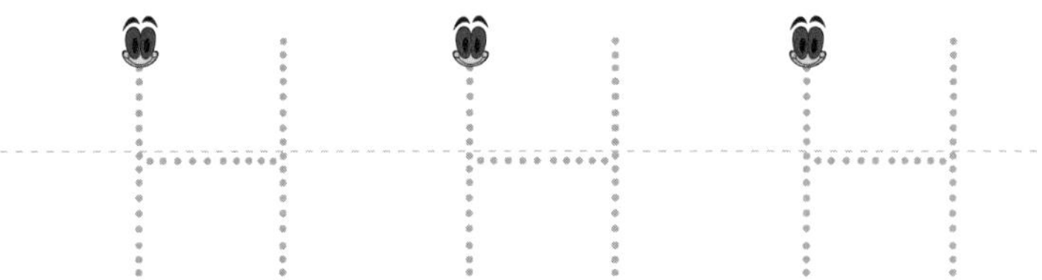

3. Now try writing it! Start with Bogart's emoji.

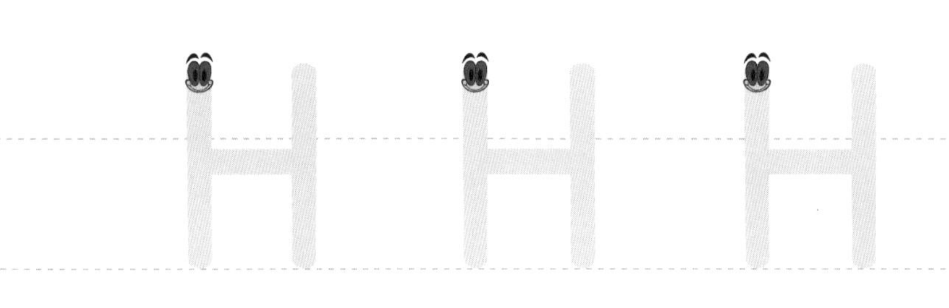

Play the sound
with the QR!

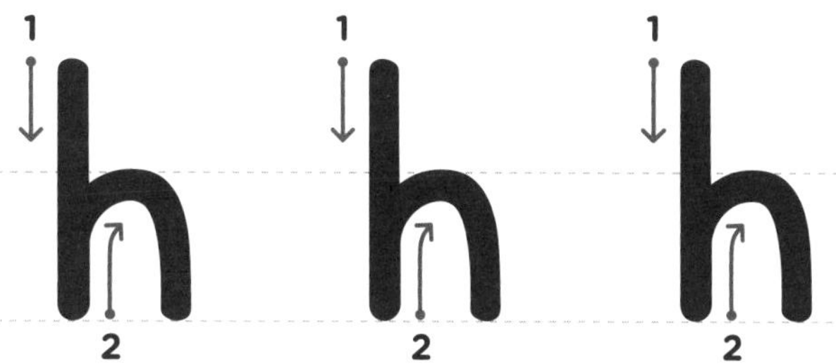
1
h
2
1
h
2
1
h
2

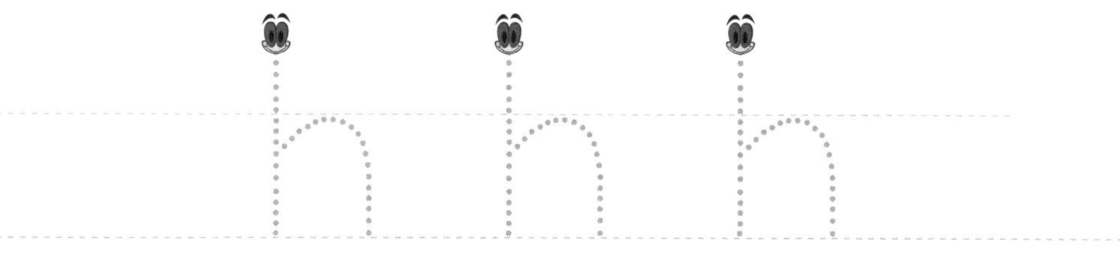

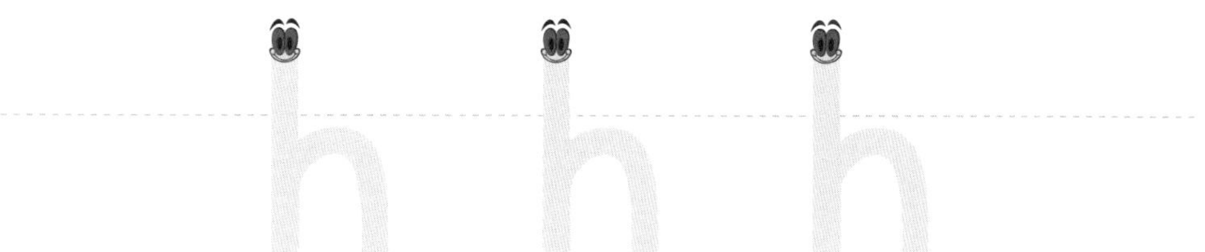

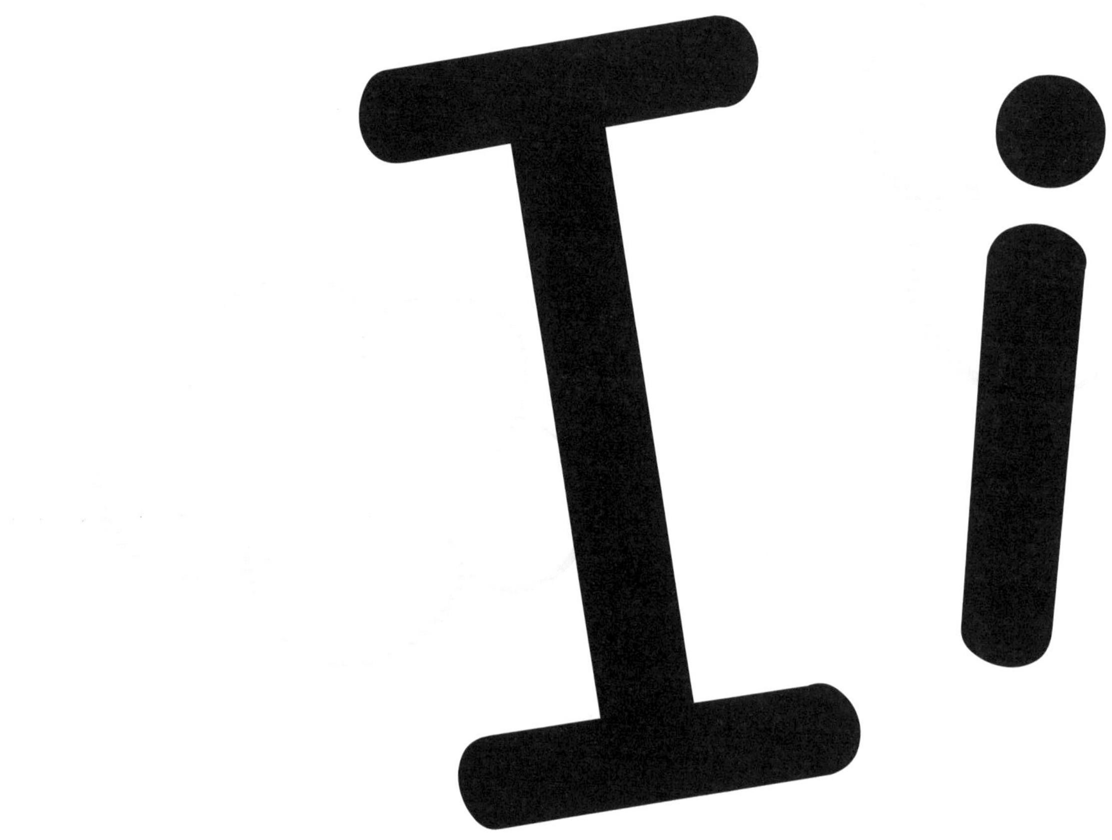

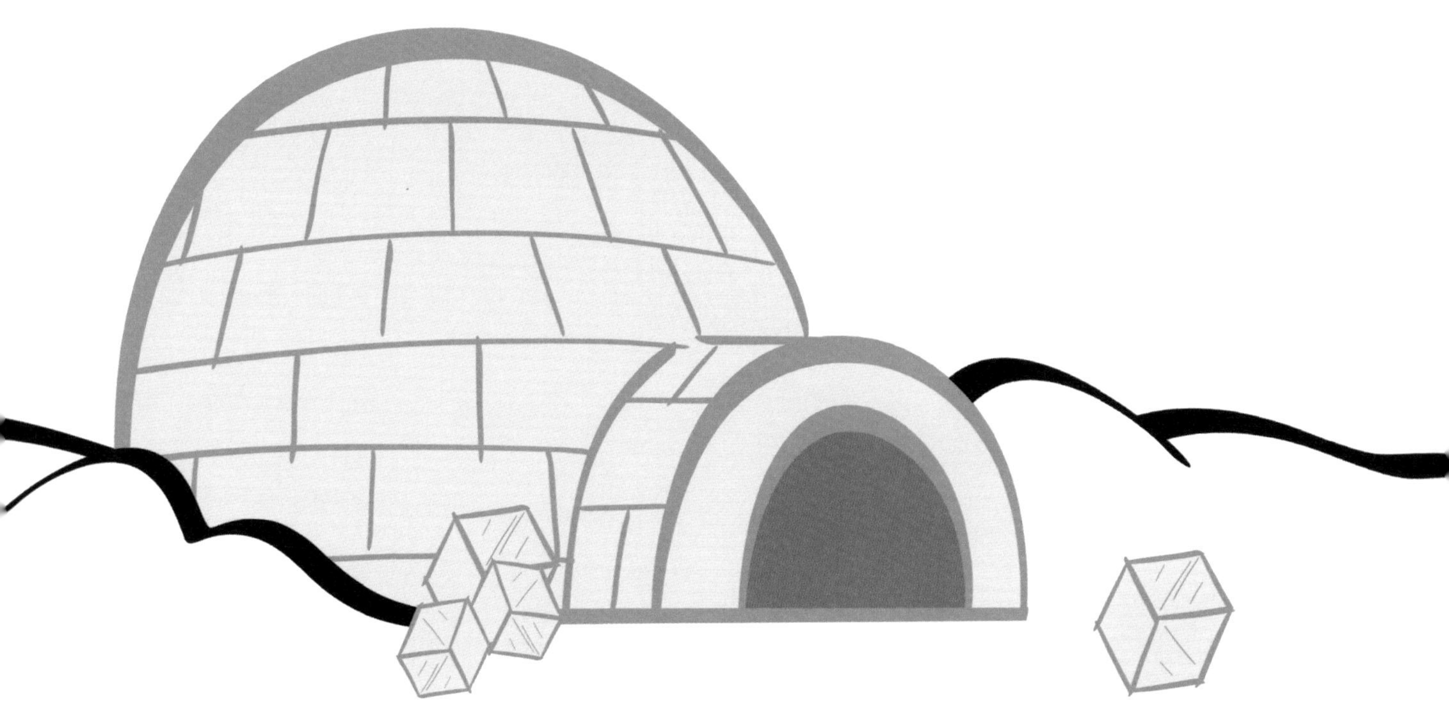

The helicopter left Bogart's throat **itchy** and sore...

He felt as **if** he couldn't eat any more.

The letter **I** is soothing and cool...

Ii

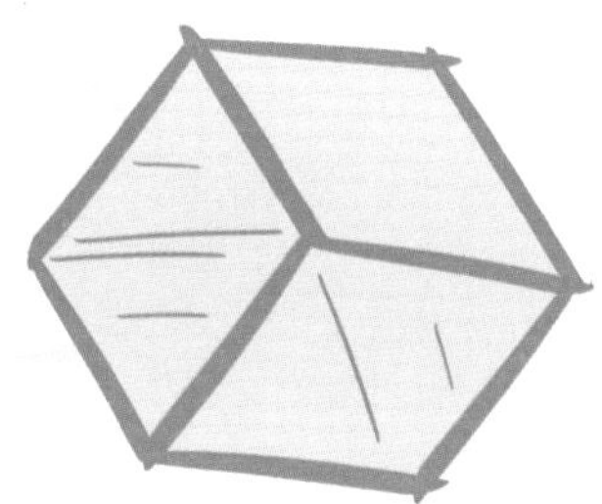

1. Follow the arrows to write the letter.

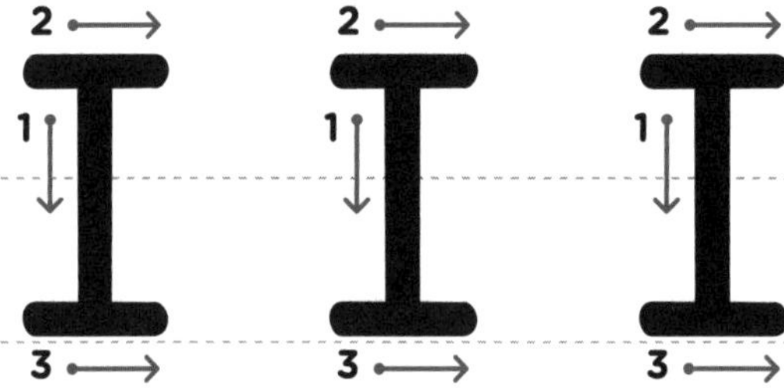

2. Trace the letter.

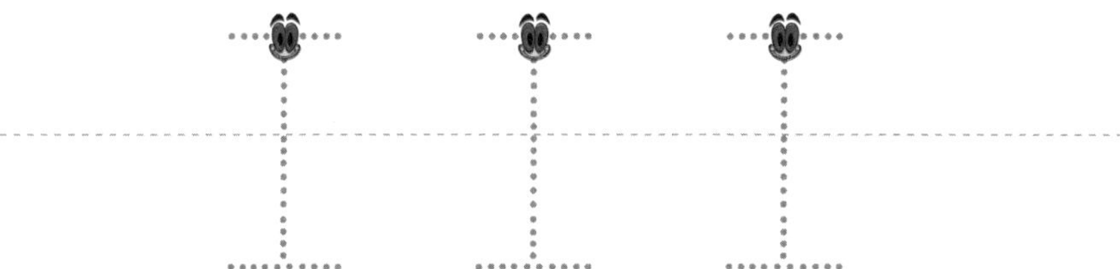

3. Now try writing it! Start with Bogart's emoji.

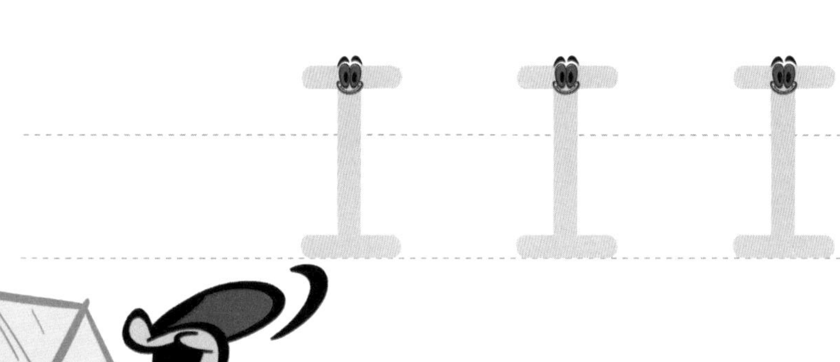

Play the sound
with the QR!

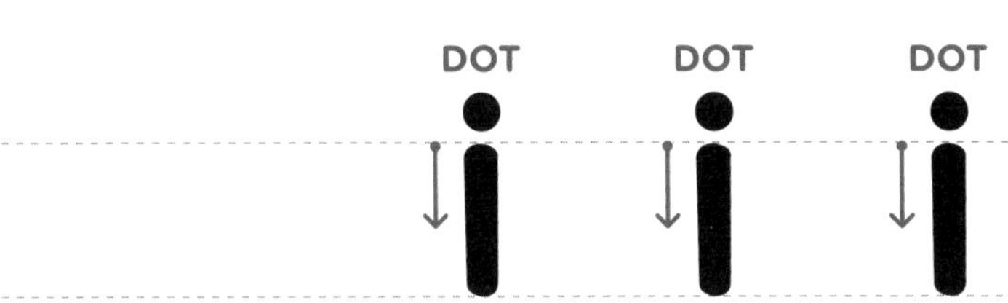
DOT
DOT
DOT

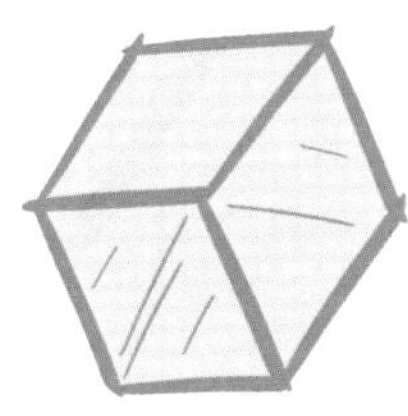

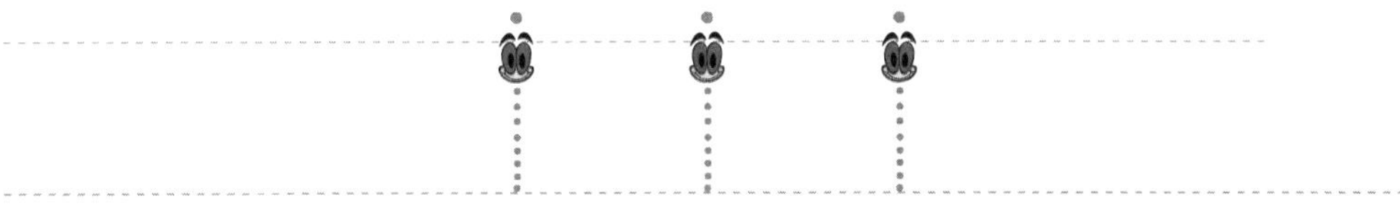

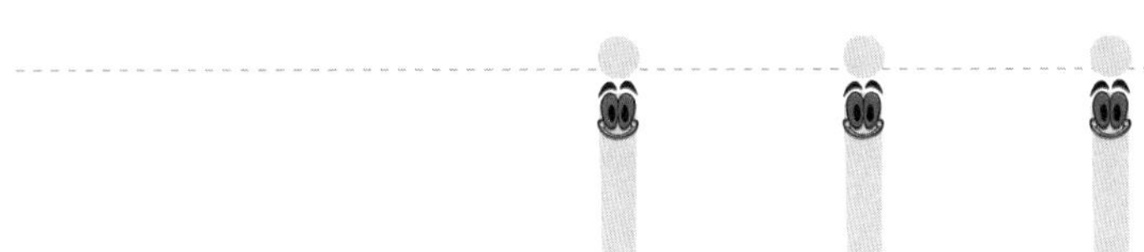

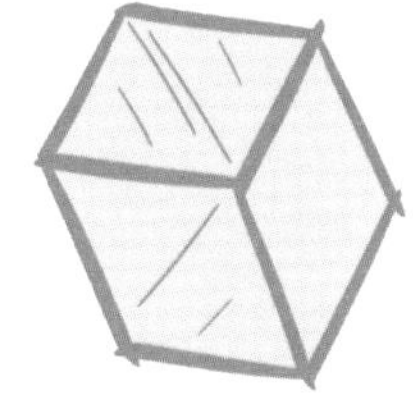

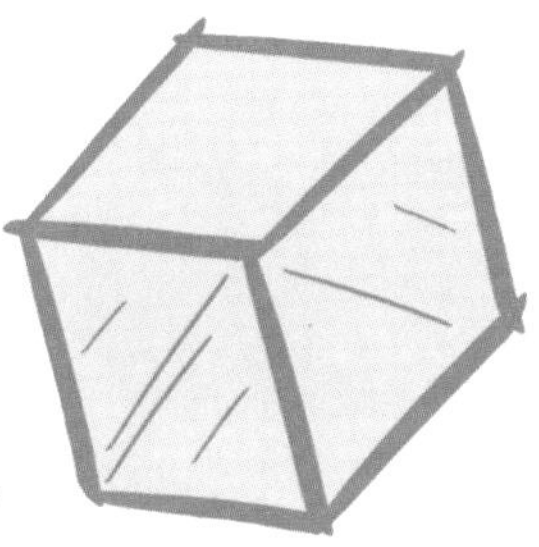

I will chomp jam.

At the letter **J**, Bogart
jumped for **joy** in gooey
purple puddles.

Jj

1. Follow the arrows to write the letter.

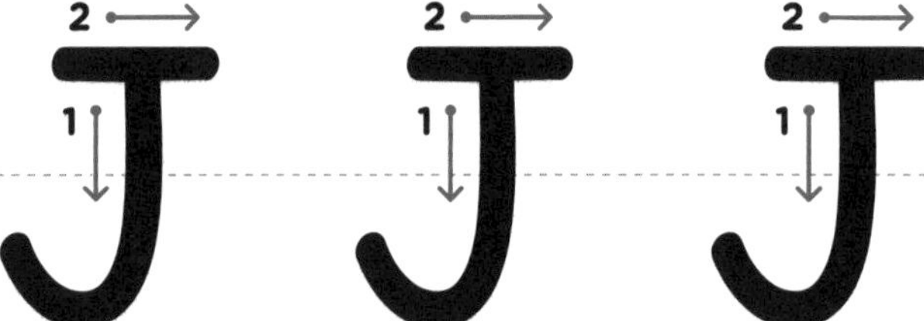

2. Trace the letter.

3. Now try writing it! Start with Bogart's emoji.

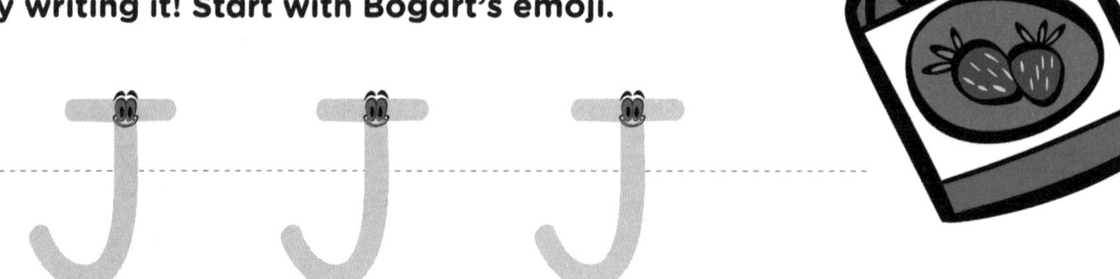

Play the sound
with the QR!
DOT
DOT
DOT

Bogart had been waiting the whole alphabet for the letter **K**.

He loved **KETCHUP**!

"And I will grow bright red butterfly wings!"

Kk

1. **Follow the arrows to write the letter.**

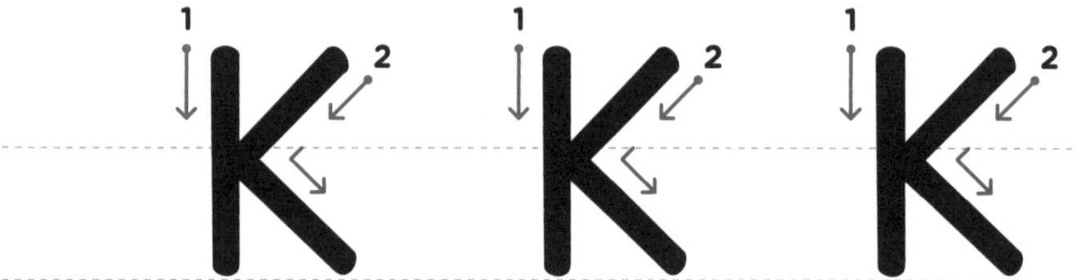

2. **Trace the letter.**

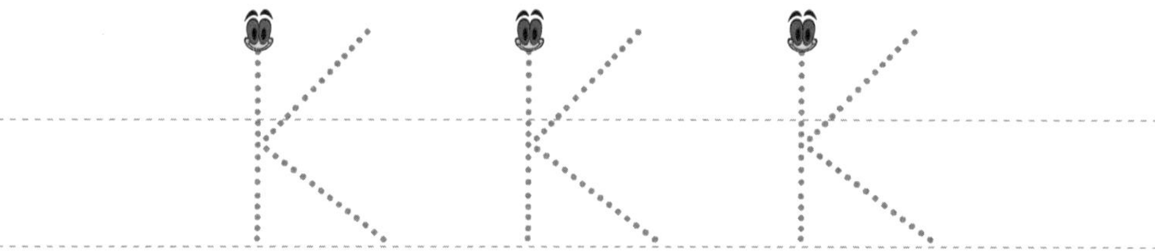

3. **Now try writing it! Start with Bogart's emoji.**

Play the sound with the QR!
1
k
2
1
k
2
1
k
2
k
k
k
k
k
k

I will chomp
lemons, lentils, and lettuce.

By the time Bogart got to **L**,
he was very, very hungry...

He chomped like a **lion**!

Ll

1. Follow the arrows to write the letter.

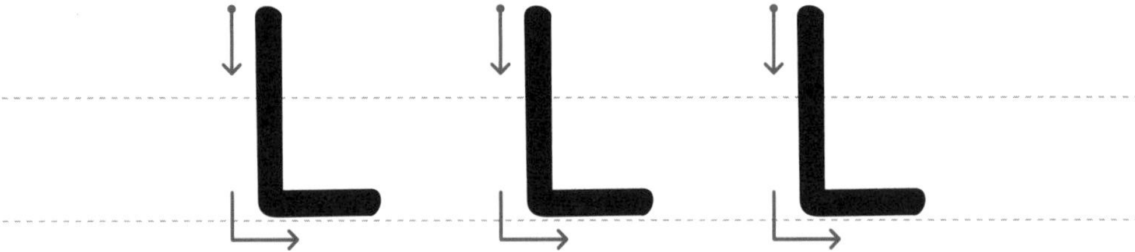

2. Trace the letter.

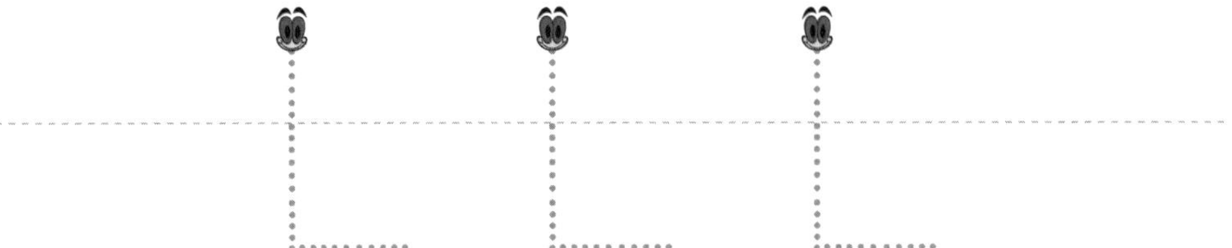

3. Now try writing it! Start with Bogart's emoji.

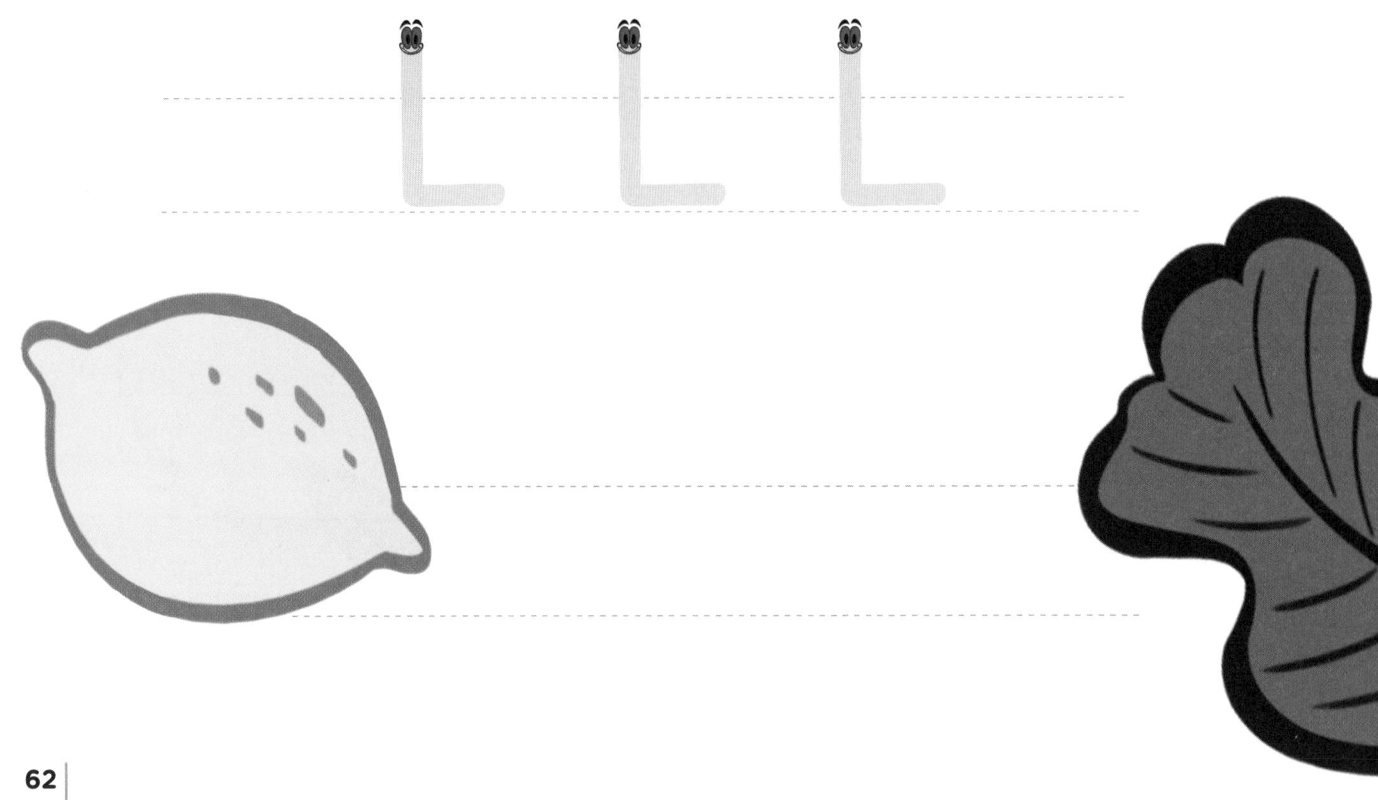

Play the sound
with the QR!

Bogart had the **munchies** for the letter **M**.

M

I will chomp
muesli with milk.
Mmmm...

Mm

1. Follow the arrows to write the letter.

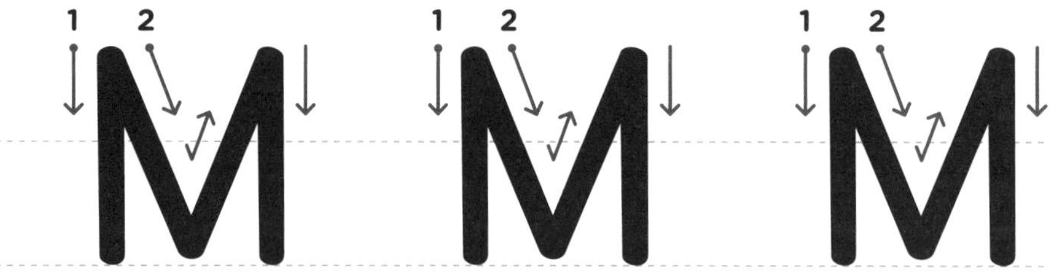

2. Trace the letter.

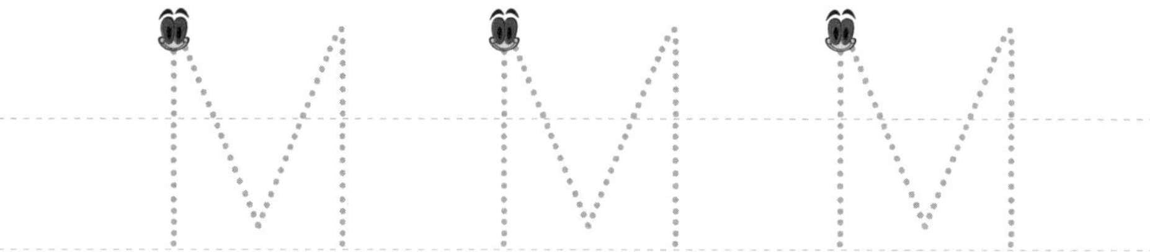

3. Now try writing it! Start with Bogart's emoji.

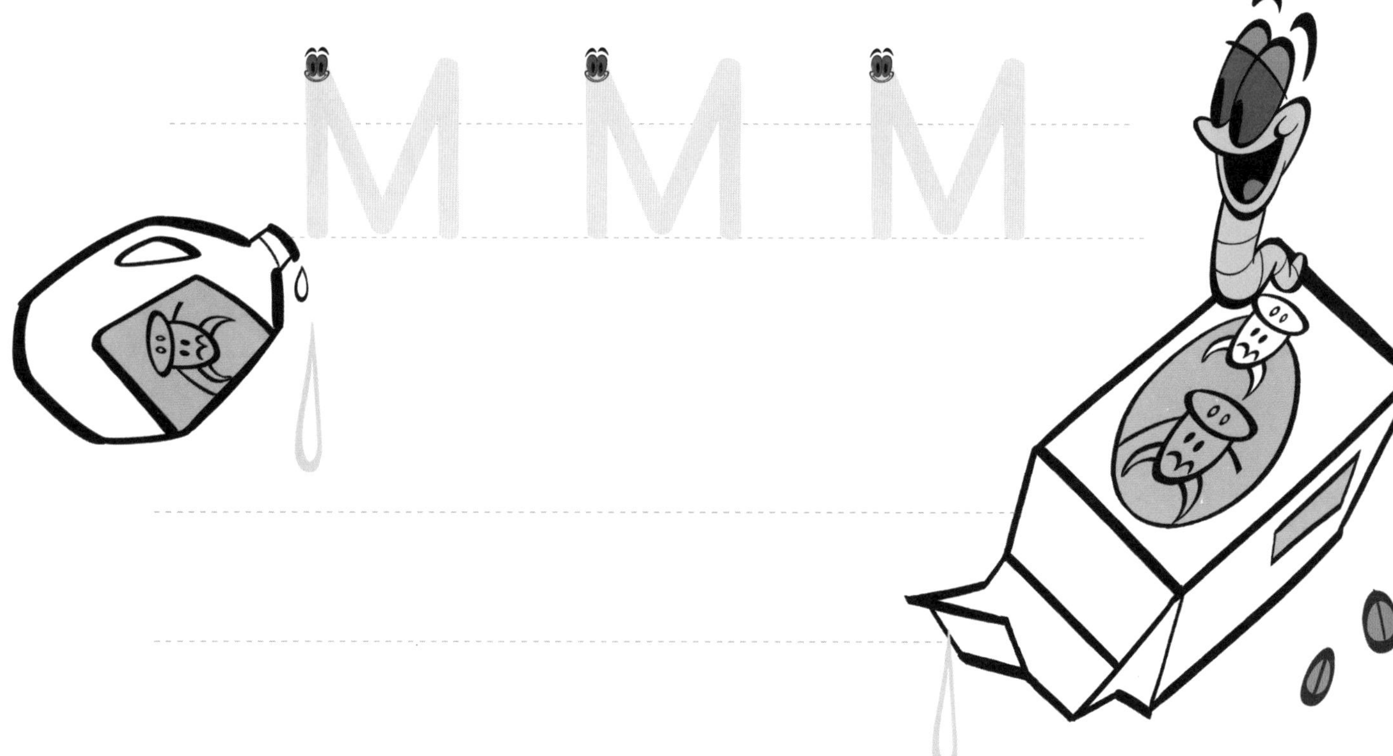

Play the sound
with the QR!
1
2 3
1
2 3
1
2 3

N

Bogart crept up behind the letter **N**.

Strong and stealthy...

"I will become a **ninja** butterfly!"

Nn

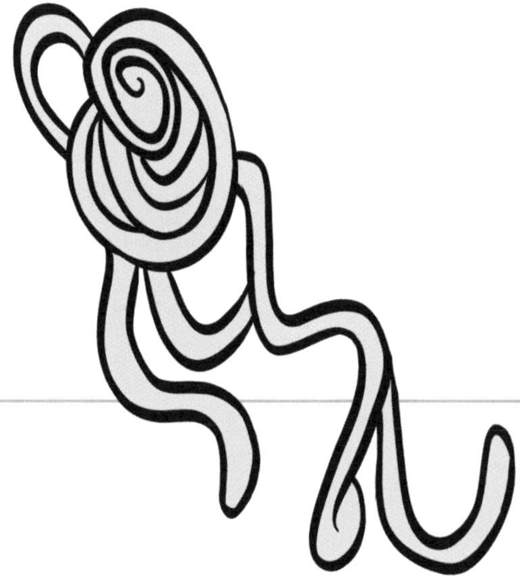

1. Follow the arrows to write the letter.

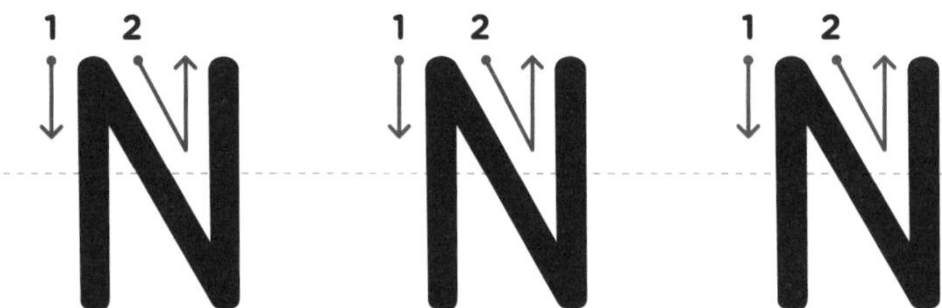

2. Trace the letter.

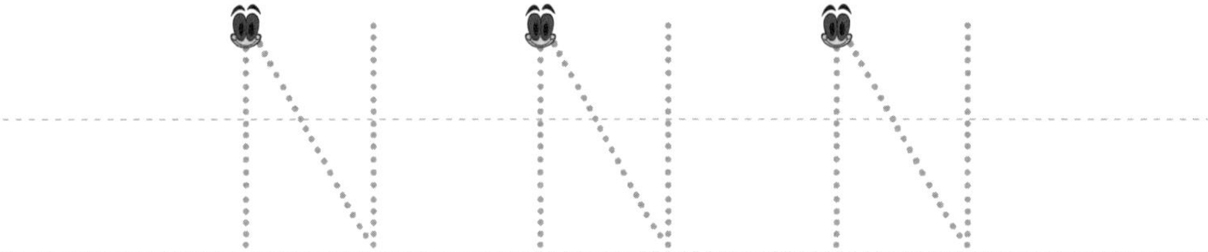

3. Now try writing it! Start with Bogart's emoji.

Play the sound
with the QR!

1
2
1
2
1
2

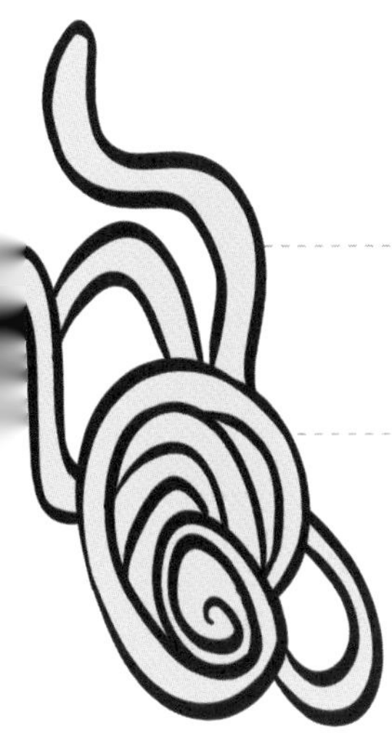

Bogart was **overjoyed**.
It's the letter **O**!

"Oooooh!"

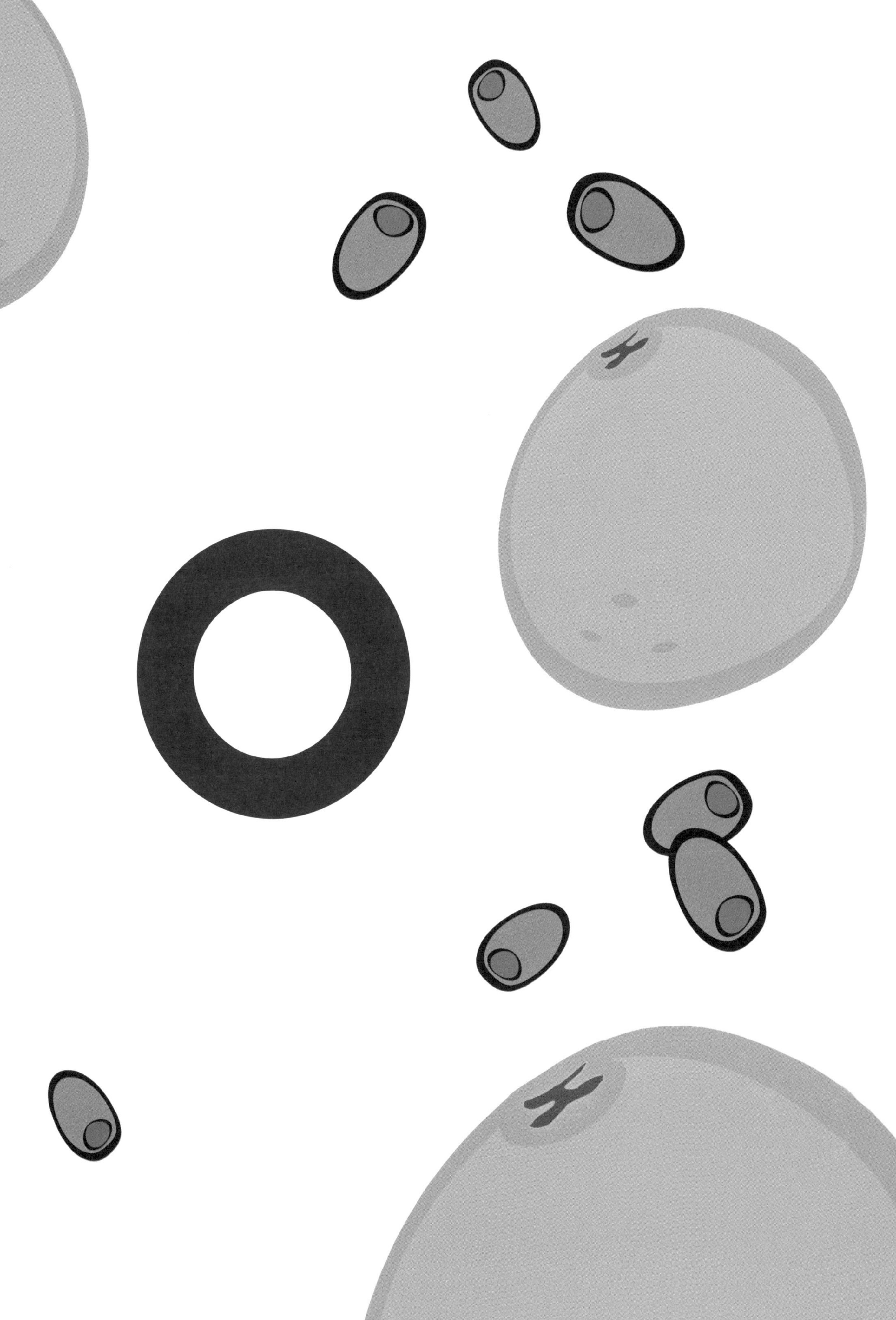

Oo

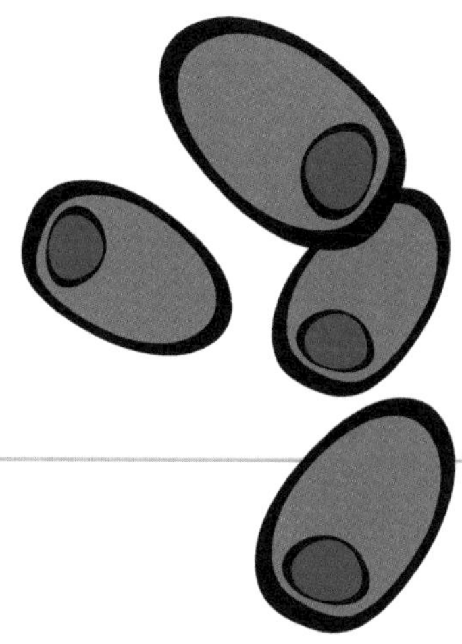

1. Follow the arrows to write the letter.

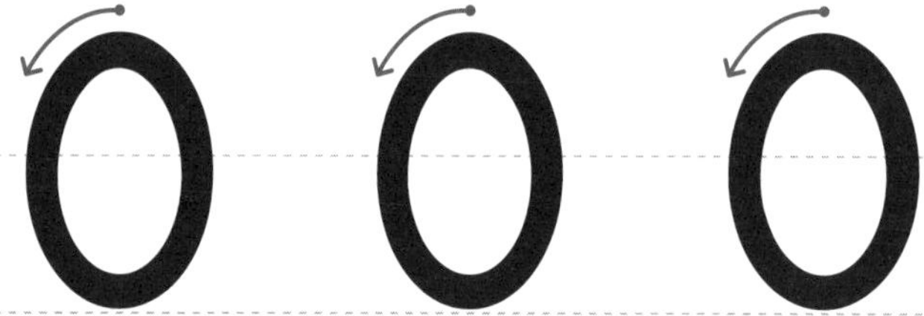

2. Trace the letter.

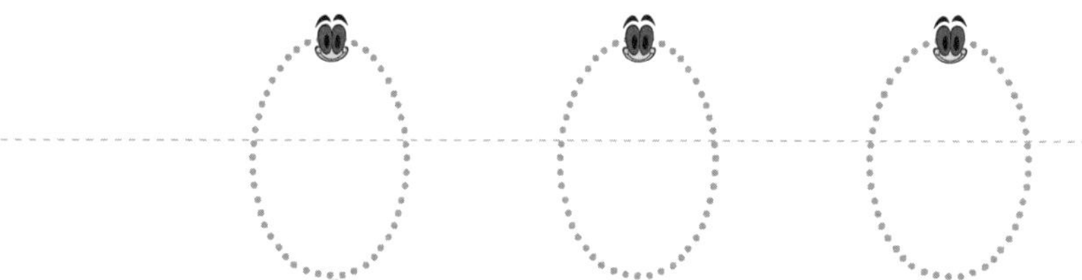

3. Now try writing it! Start with Bogart's emoji.

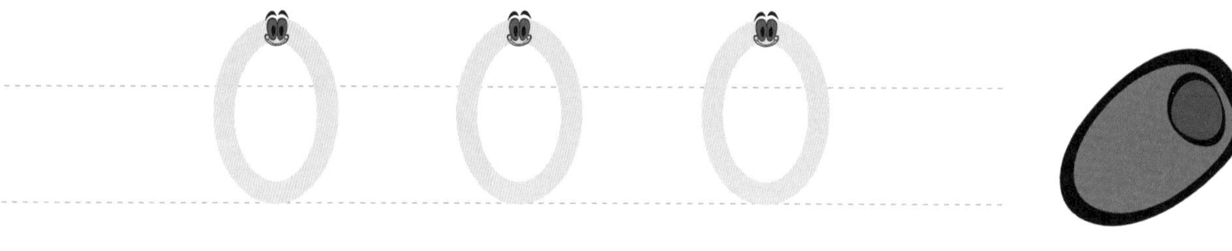

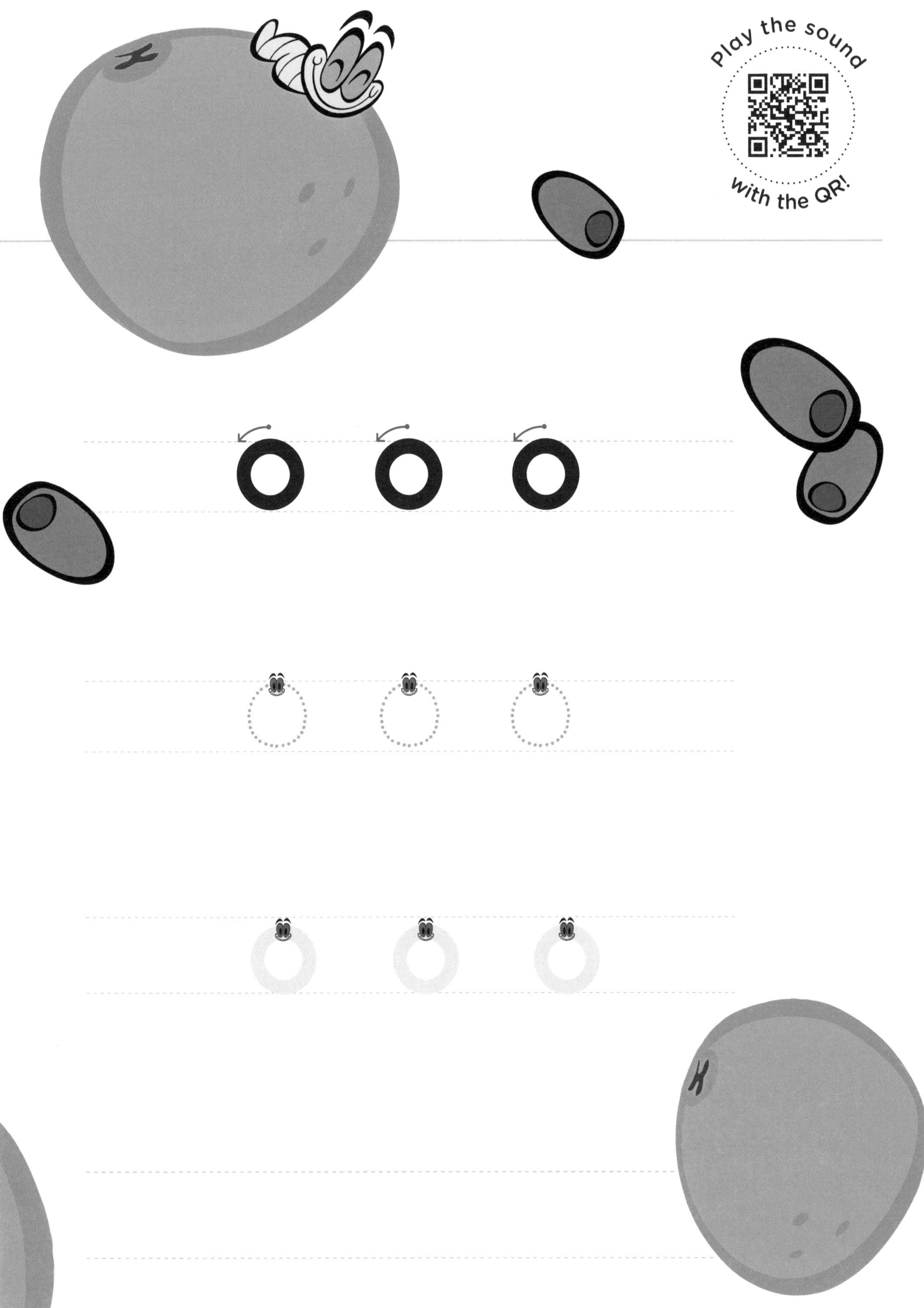
Play the sound
with the QR!

At the letter **P**, a familiar smell wafted through the air.

Bogart couldn't help himself!

It was a
poo-fect day.

Pp

1. Follow the arrows to write the letter.

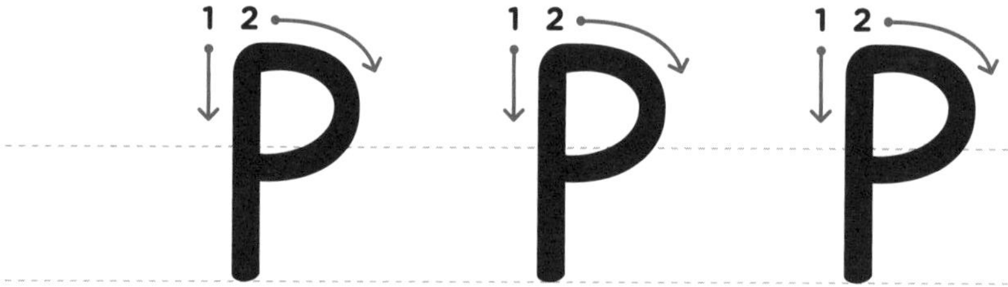

2. Trace the letter.

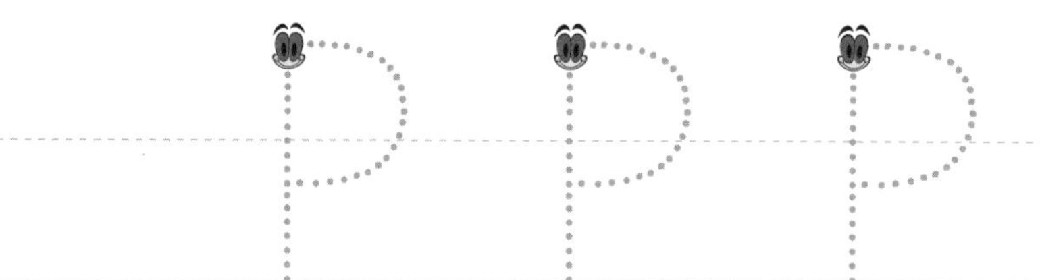

3. Now try writing it! Start with Bogart's emoji.

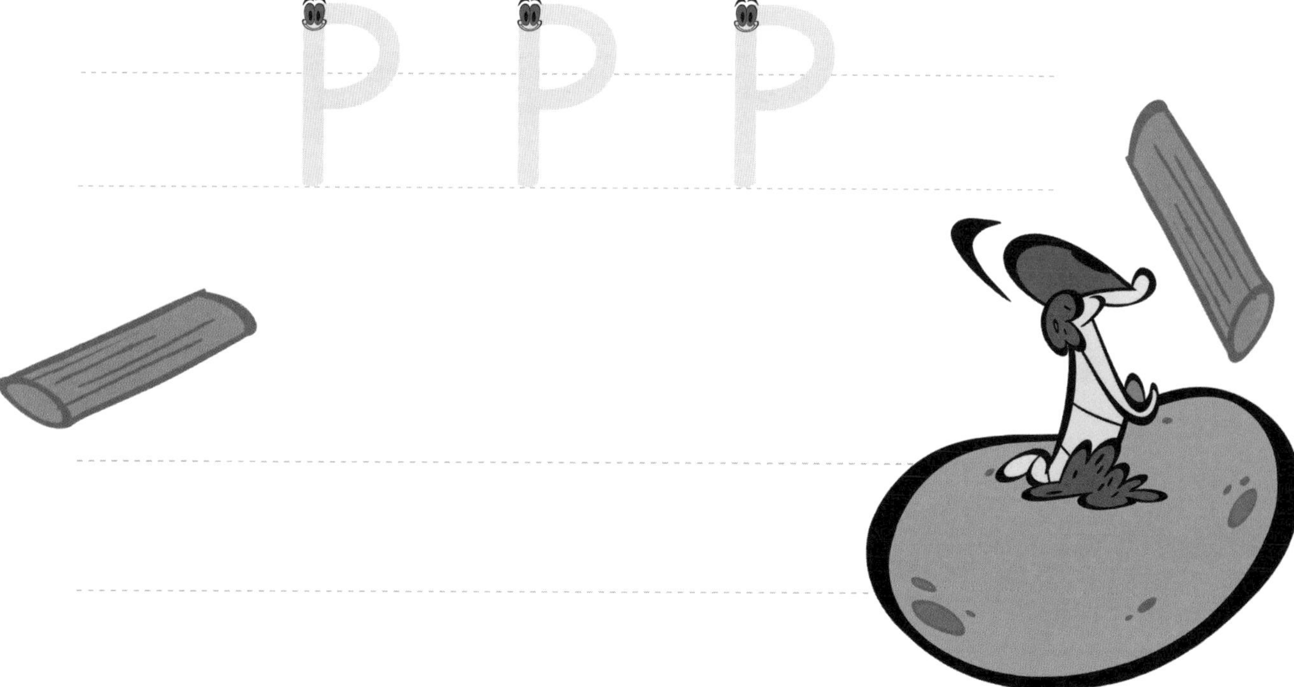

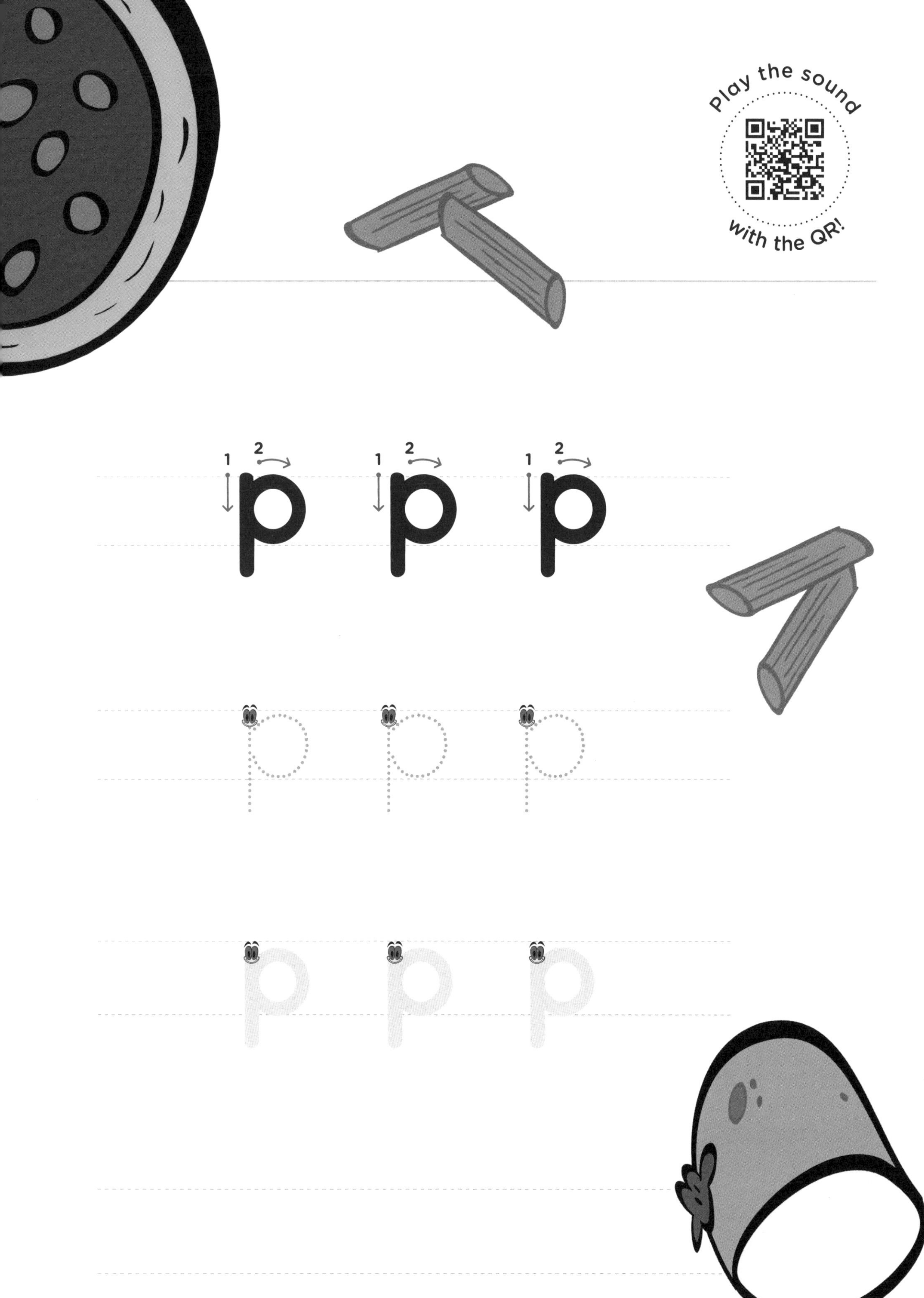
Play the sound
with the QR!
1
2
p p p

Bogart ran after the letter **Q**.

But the little duckies
were too **quick**. Phew!

Qq

1. Follow the arrows to write the letter.

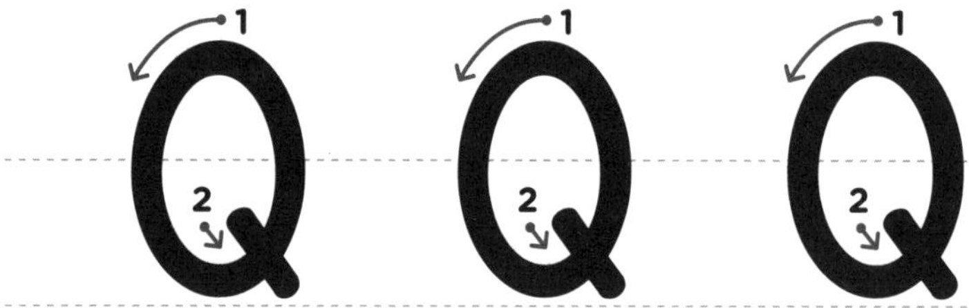

2. Trace the letter.

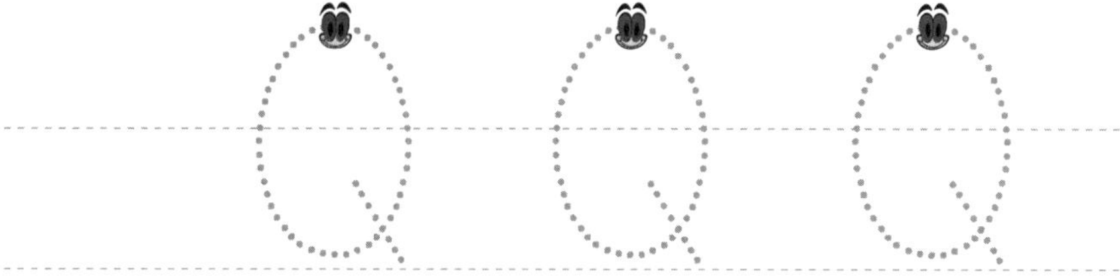

3. Now try writing it! Start with Bogart's emoji.

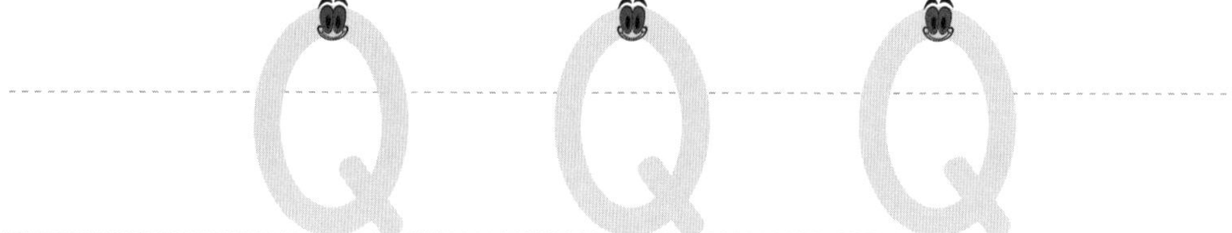

Quack!

q q q

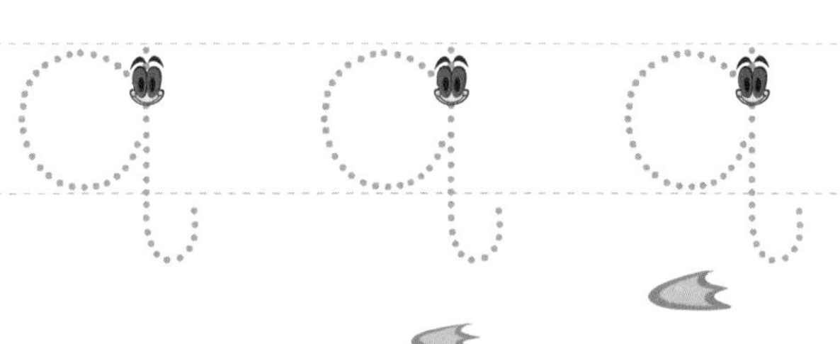

At the letter **R**, Bogart began to spin in circles.

Round and **round**,
he spun across the sky...

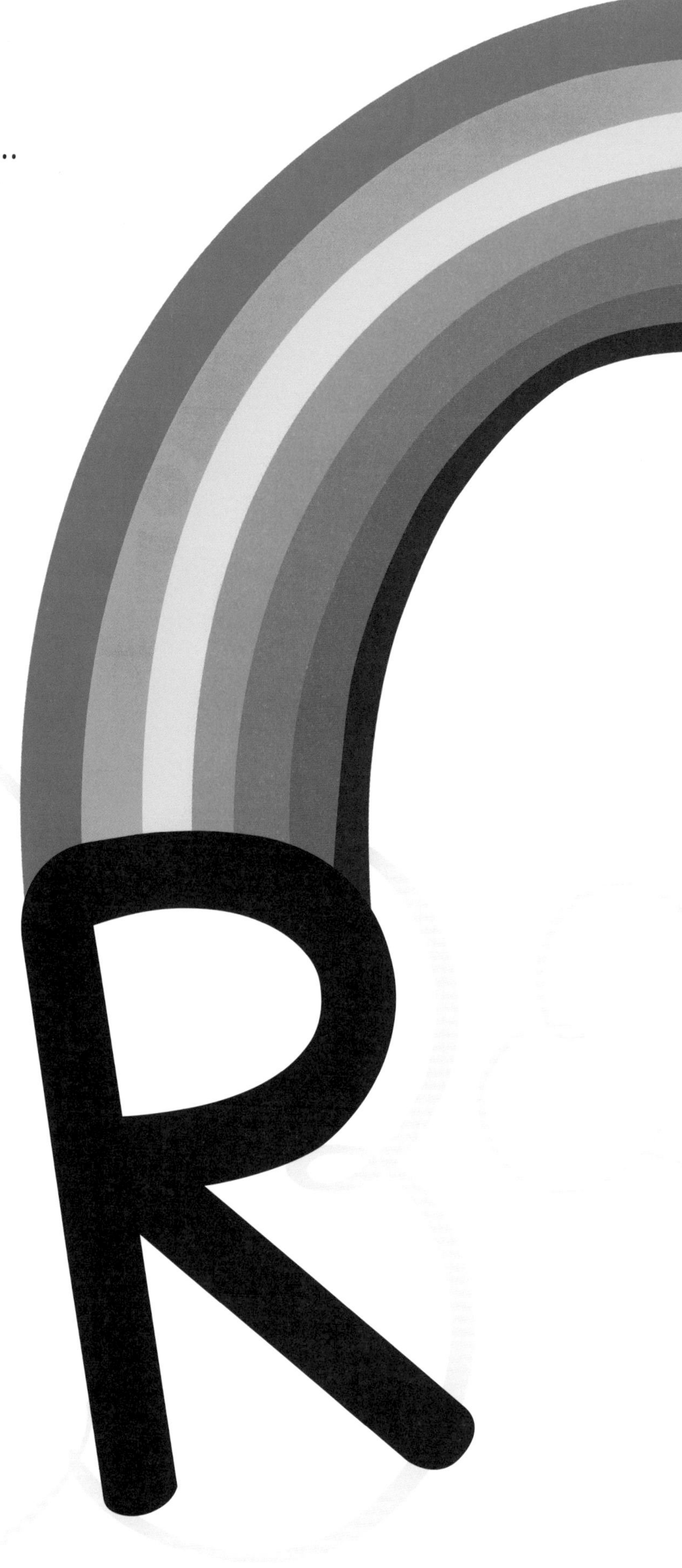

And over the **rainbow**,
he flew so high.

Rr

1. Follow the arrows to write the letter.

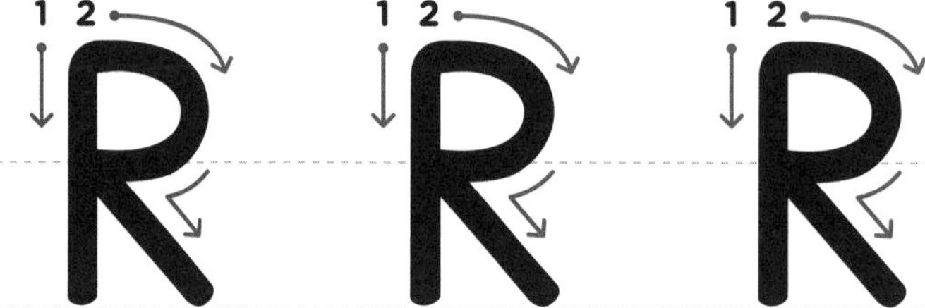

2. Trace the letter.

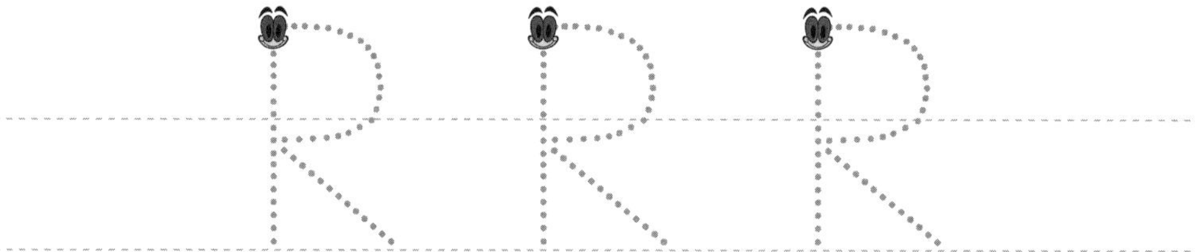

3. Now try writing it! Start with Bogart's emoji.

Play the sound
with the QR!

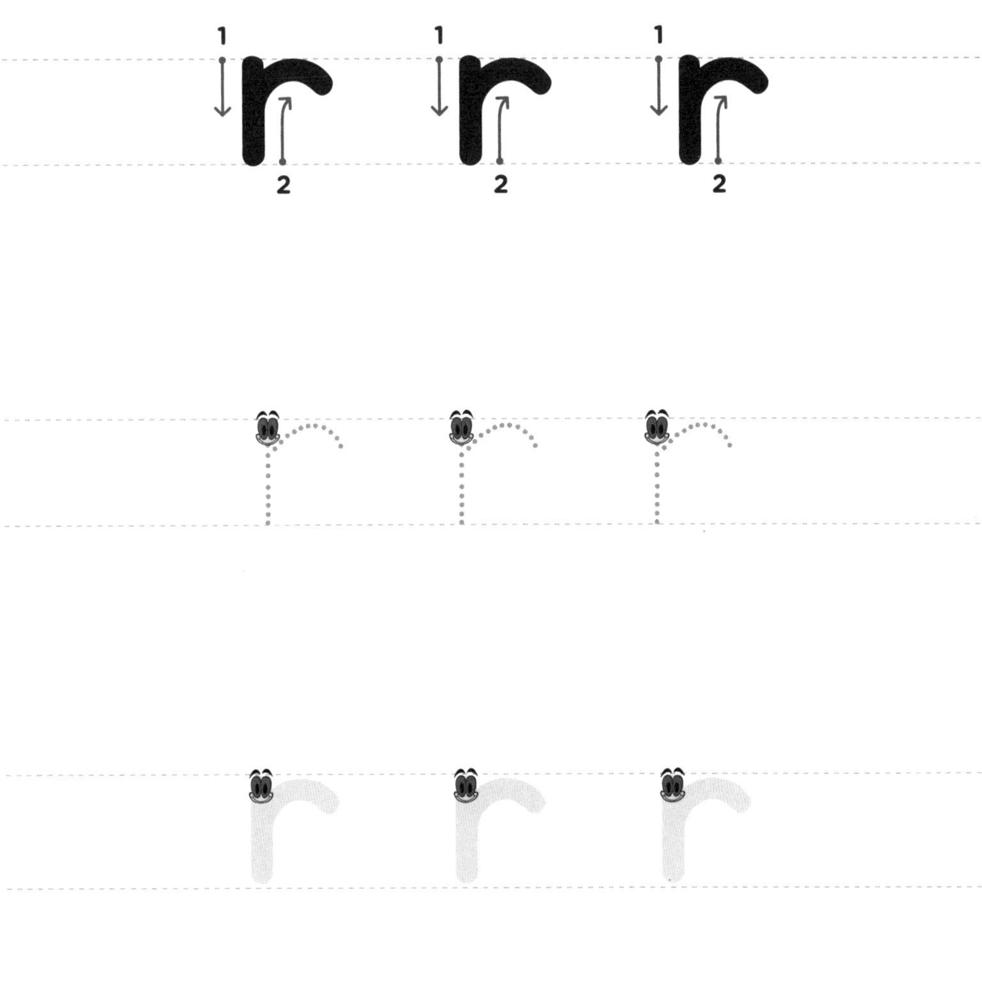
1
2
1
2
1
2

The letter **S** made Bogart **salivate**.

And he **slurped** up every last bite.

Ss

1. Follow the arrows to write the letter.

2. Trace the letter.

3. Now try writing it! Start with Bogart's emoji.

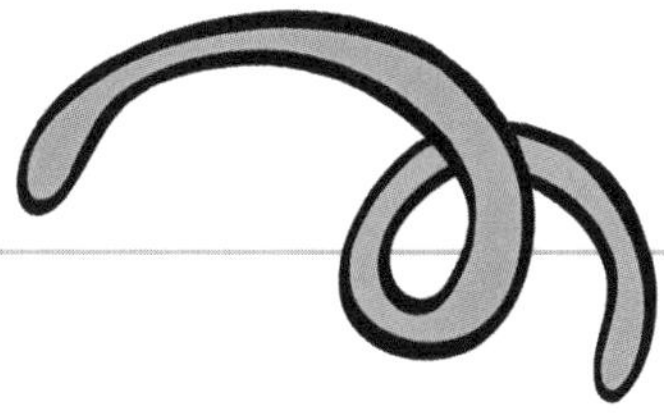

Play the sound with the QR!

s s s

s s s

s s s

Tea-time!
It's time for **T**!

Careful what you chomp, Bogart!
Or you might turn into a firefly,
not a butterfly.

Tt

1. Follow the arrows to write the letter.

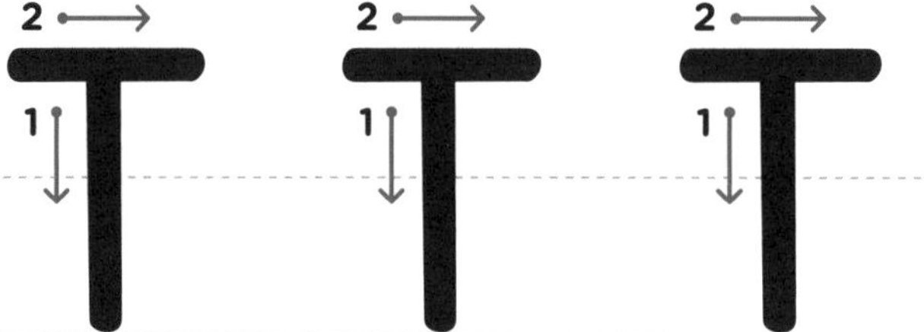

2. Trace the letter.

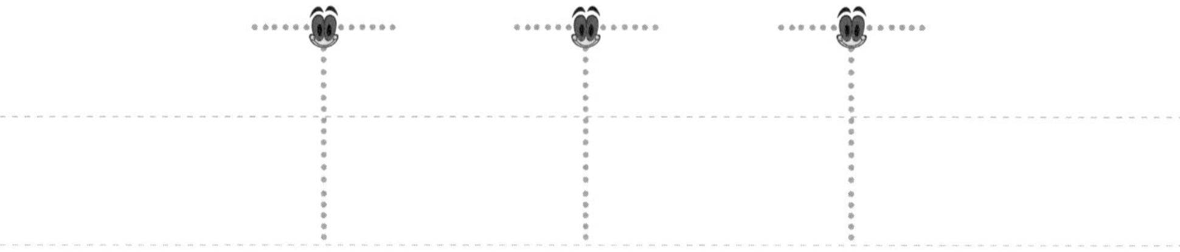

3. Now try writing it! Start with Bogart's emoji.

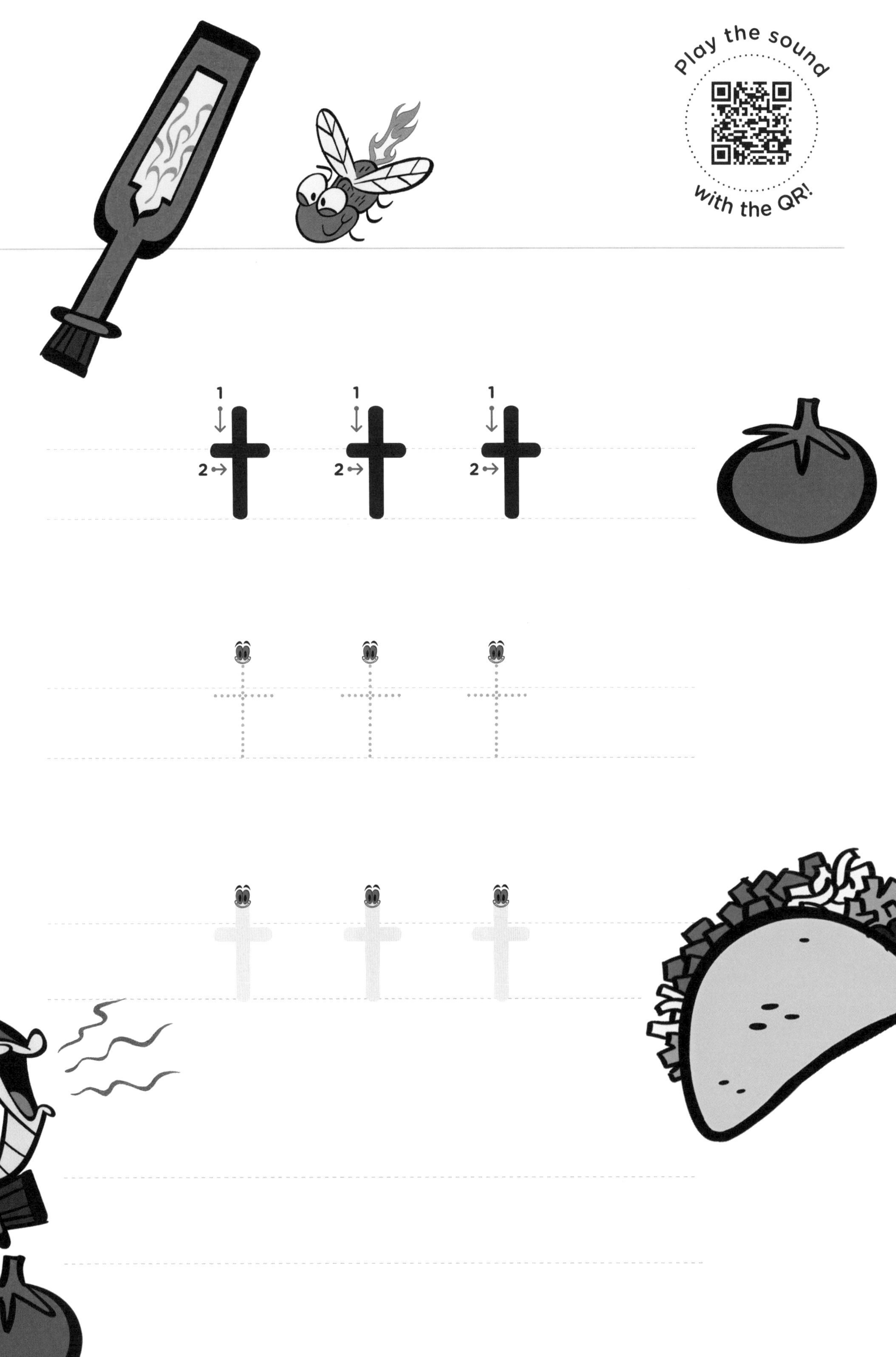
Play the sound
with the QR!
1
2
1
2
1
2

When Bogart reached the letter **U**, the sky grew dark, and black, and blue.

The rain started pouring, but Bogart was prepared for any weather...

I will chomp
through an umbrella!

Uu

1. Follow the arrows to write the letter.

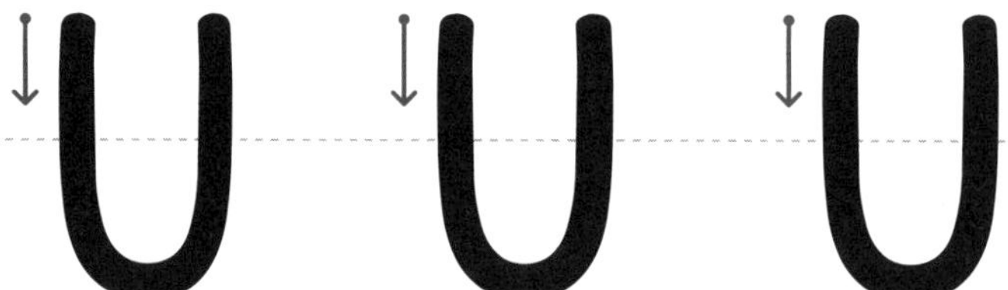

2. Trace the letter.

3. Now try writing it! Start with Bogart's emoji.

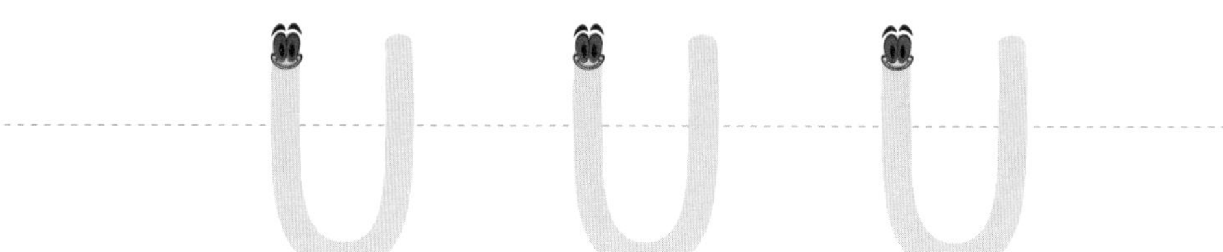

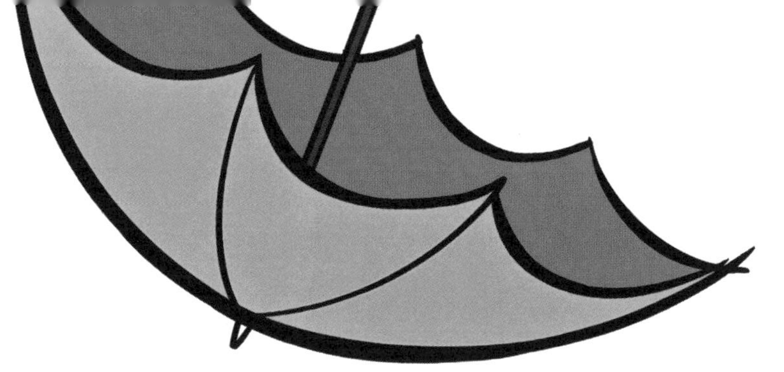

Play the sound
with the QR!

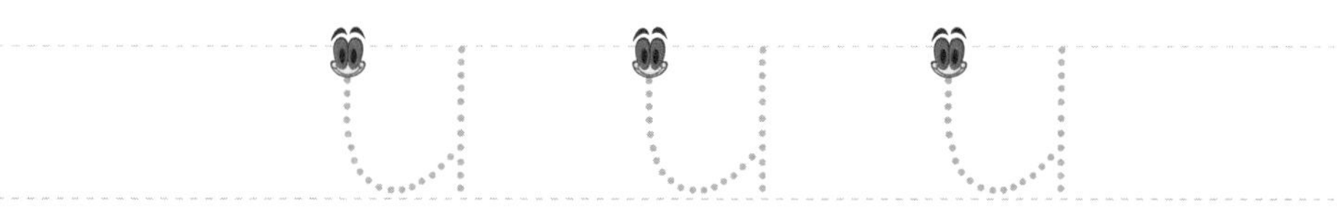
1
2
1
2
1
2

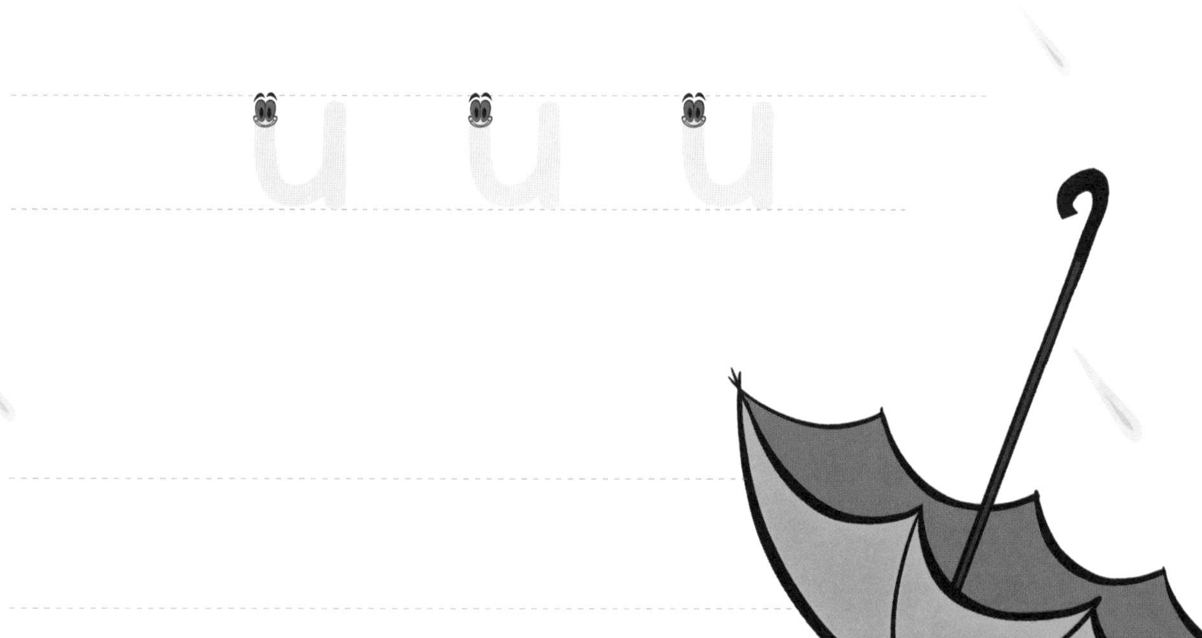

At the letter **V**,
Bogart decided he wanted
to be a healthy butterfly!

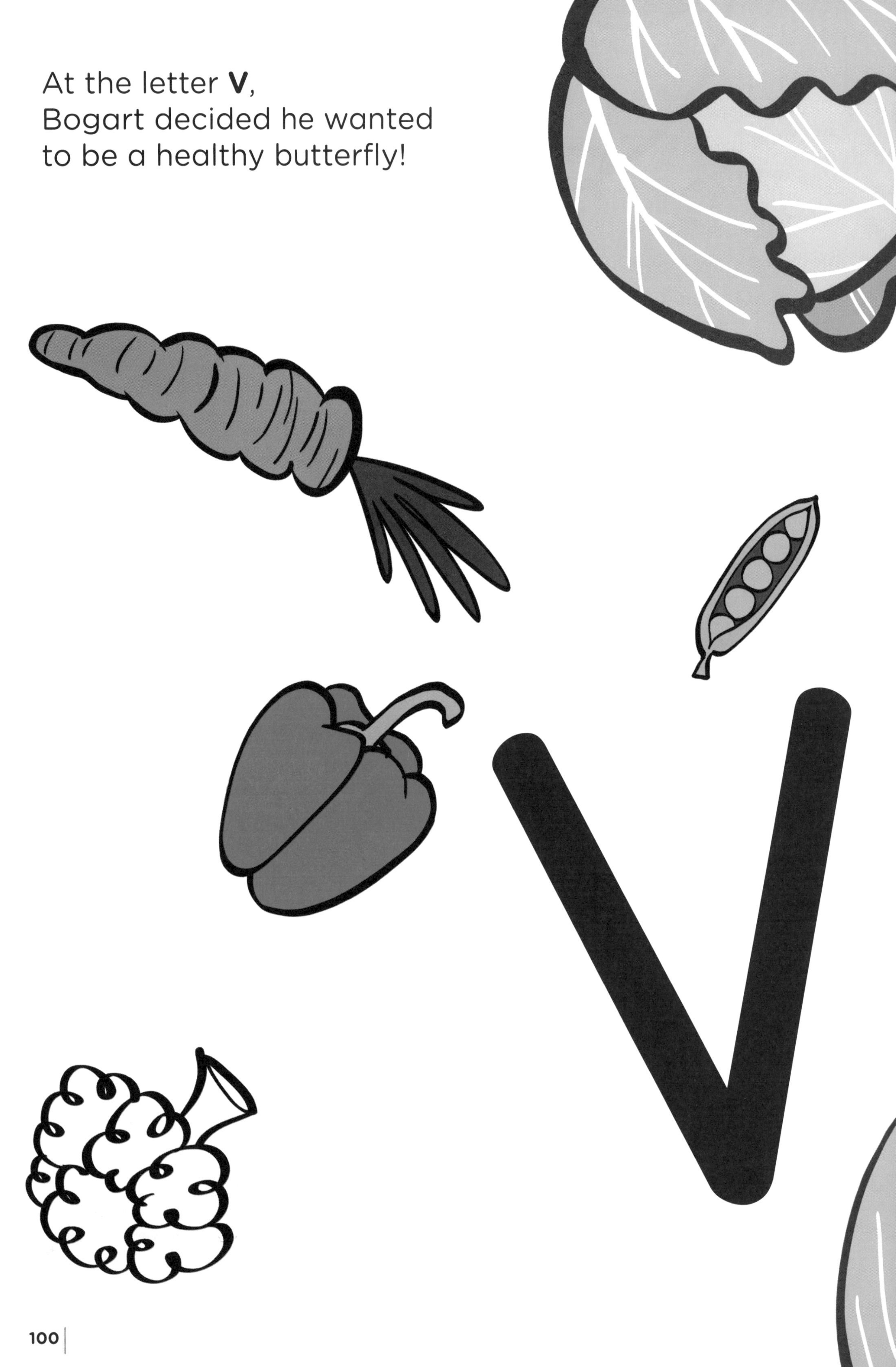

I will chomp
lots and lots and lots and lots of vegetables.
V

1. Follow the arrows to write the letter.

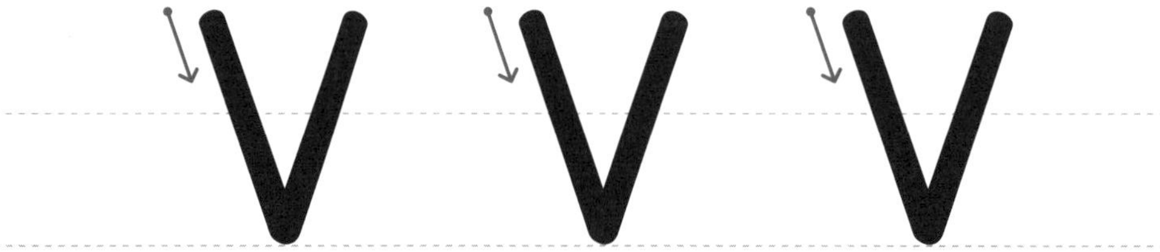

2. Trace the letter.

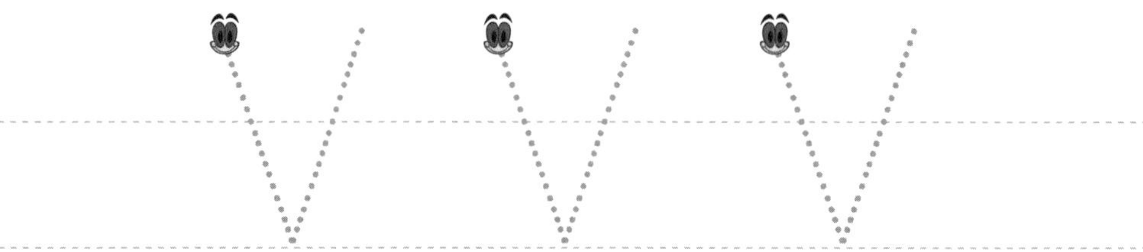

3. Now try writing it! Start with Bogart's emoji.

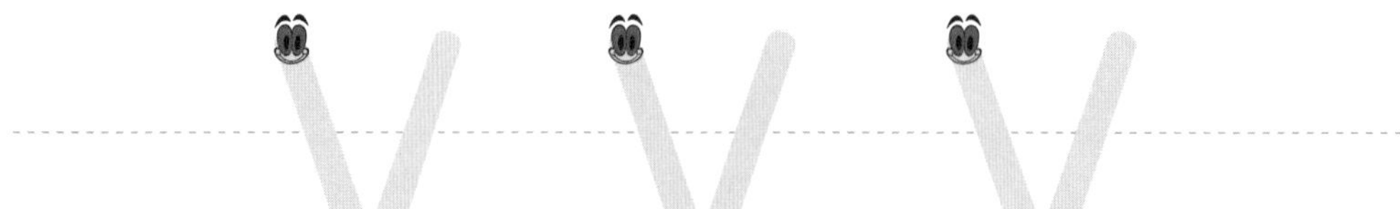

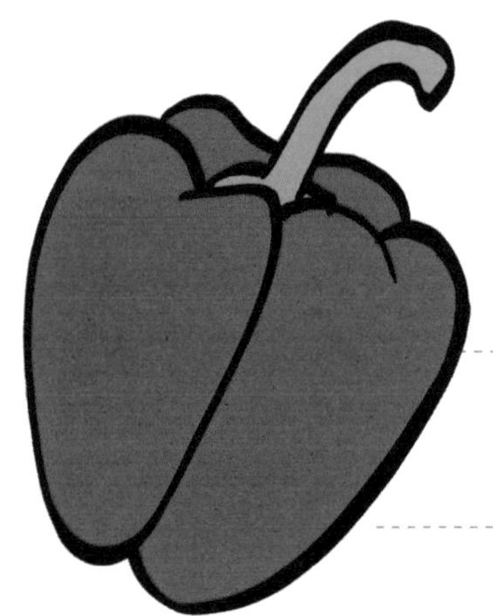

Play the sound
with the QR!
v v v

Bogart **wanted** to fly like the **wind**!

Wahoo! The letter **W**!

I will chomp
waffles, walnuts, and watermelons.
W

Ww

1. Follow the arrows to write the letter.

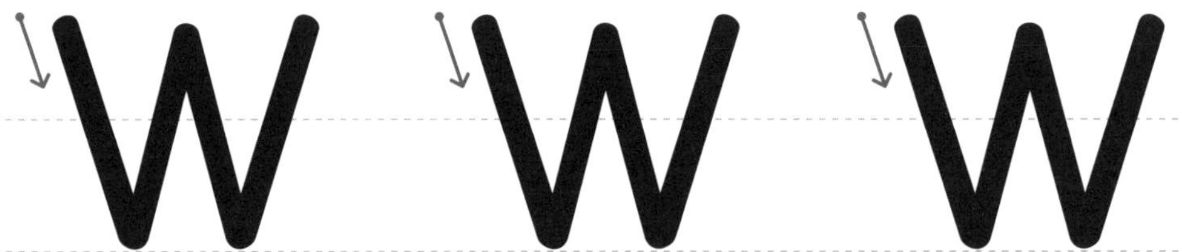

2. Trace the letter.

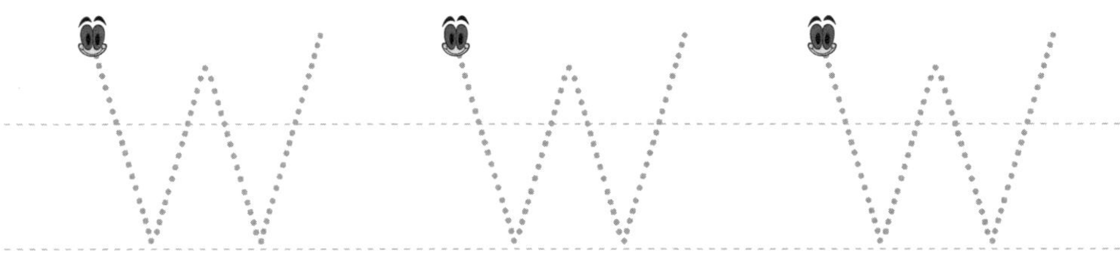

3. Now try writing it! Start with Bogart's emoji.

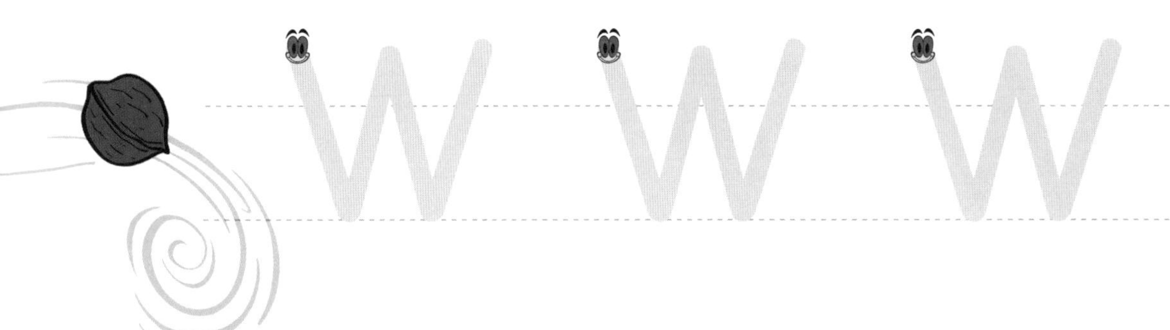

Play the sound
with the QR!
w w w
w w w
w w w

The letter **X** is unusual, extra special, and musical!

But something didn't sound right. Bogart gasped, and groaned, and grumbled. His tummy was all jumbled.

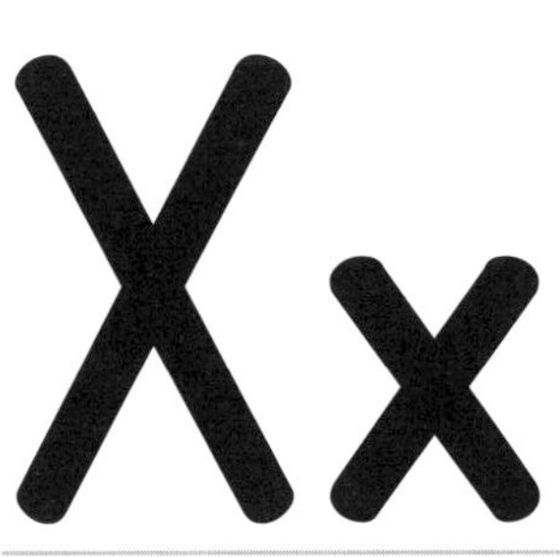

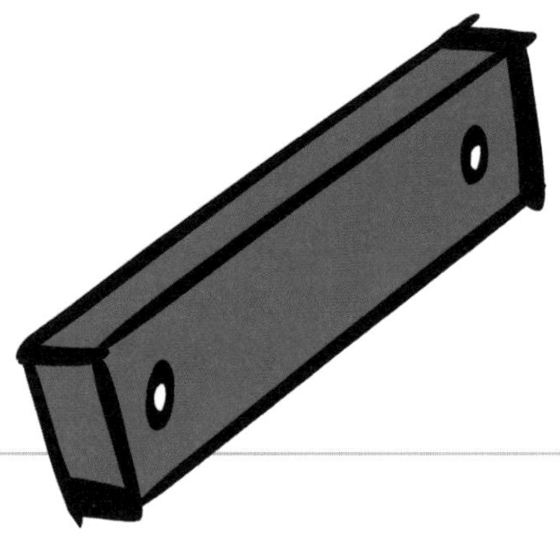

1. Follow the arrows to write the letter.

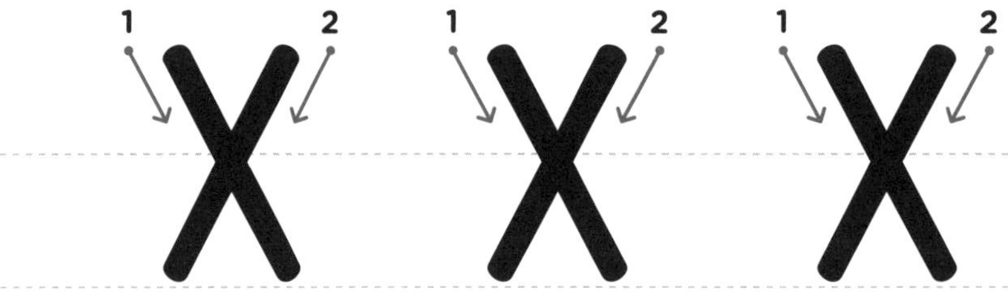

2. Trace the letter.

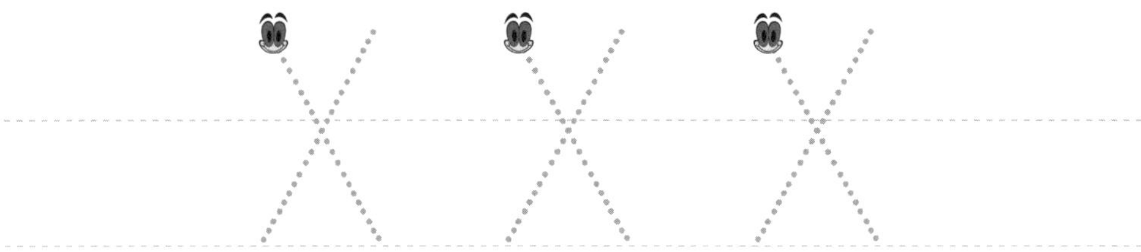

3. Now try writing it! Start with Bogart's emoji.

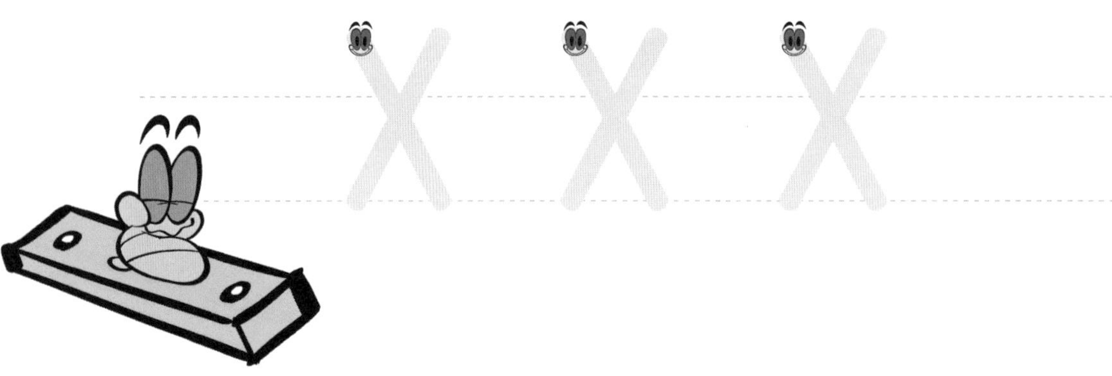

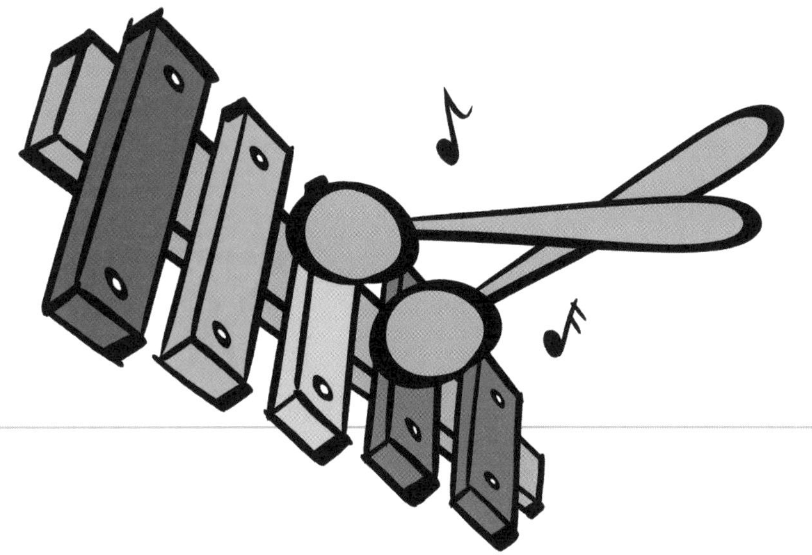

Play the sound
with the QR!

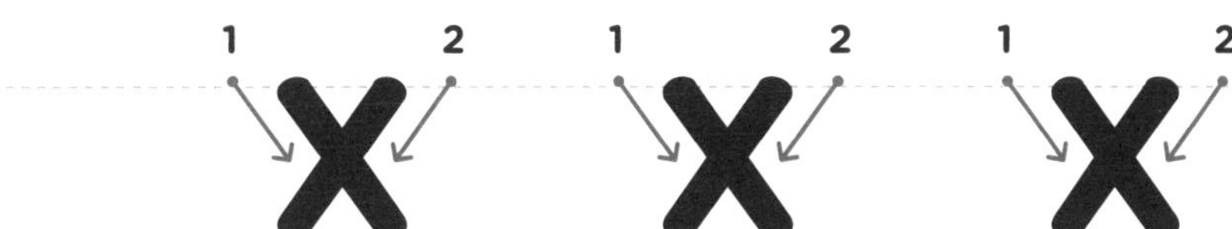
1 x 2
1 x 2
1 x 2

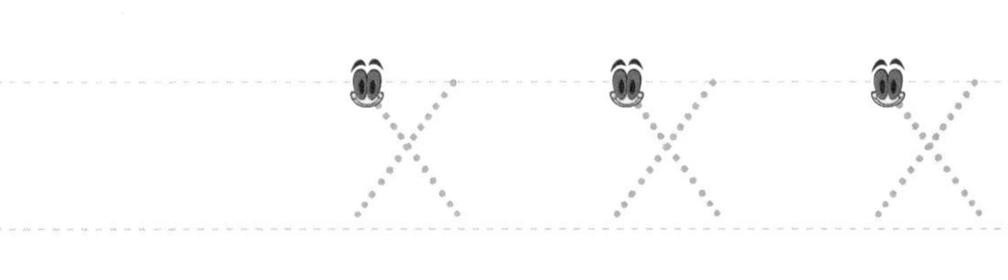

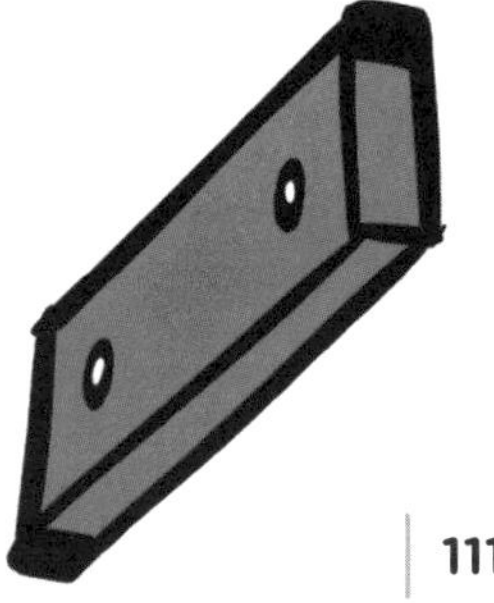

My, oh my – it's the letter **Y**!
Bogart needed something **yummy**...

To settle the music coming
from his tummy.

I will
chomp
lots and lots
of **yogurt**.
y

Yy

1. Follow the arrows to write the letter.

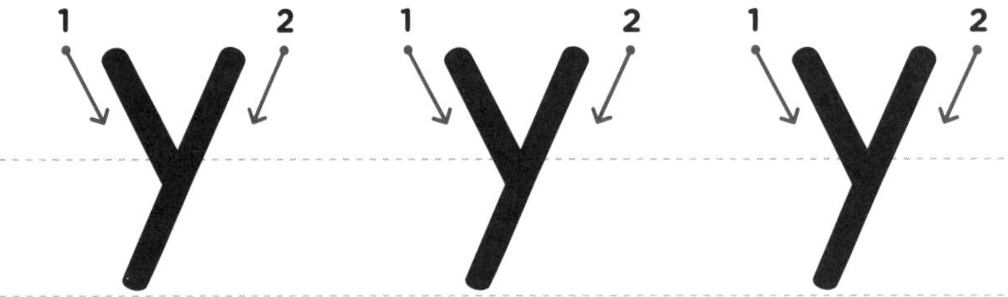

2. Trace the letter.

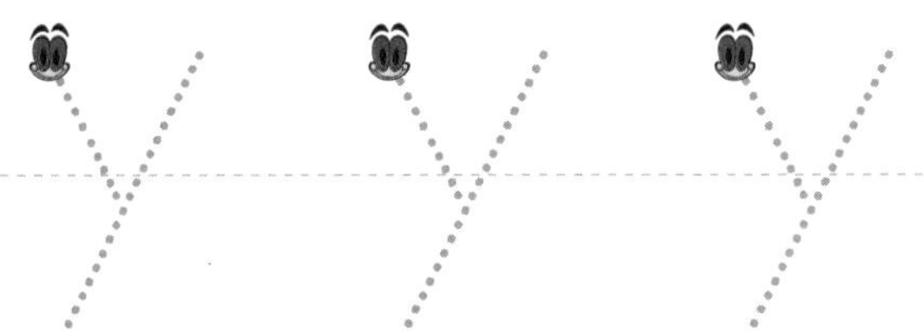

3. Now try writing it! Start with Bogart's emoji.

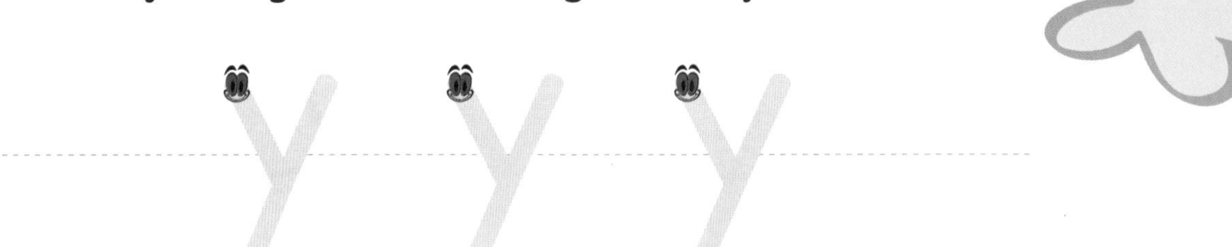

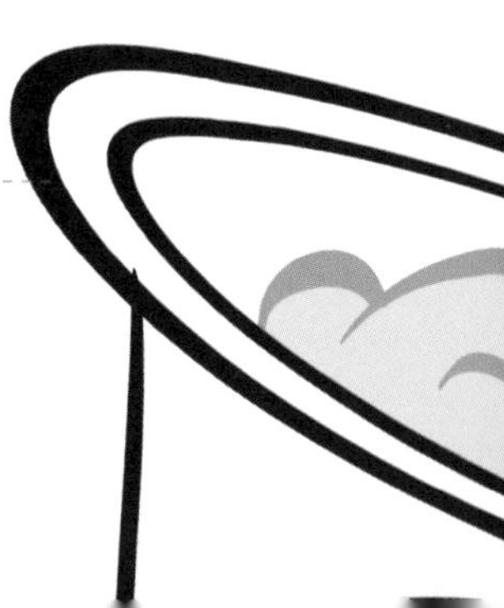

1 y 2   1 y 2   1 y 2

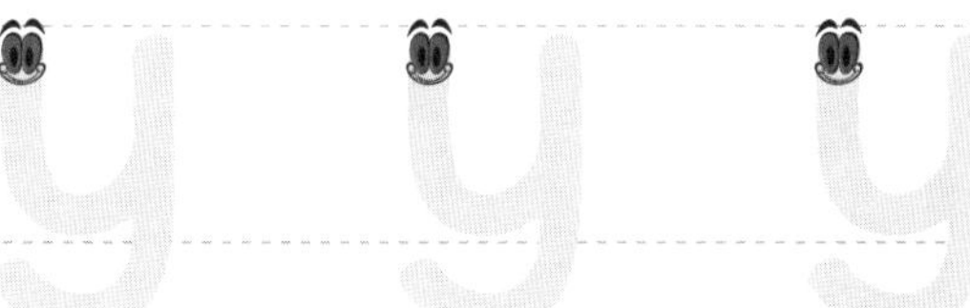

Finally, the letter **Z**.

Bogart had chomped, chewed, and crunched his way to the end of the alphabet.

He wasn't a tiny baby fly anymore.

He was big, and fat, and full.

Tired, he took a nap.
"**Zzzz**," he snored.

Bogart had a magical dream...

Of butterfly wings and flying high.

Of **zig-zagging** and **zooming** through the sky...

Zz

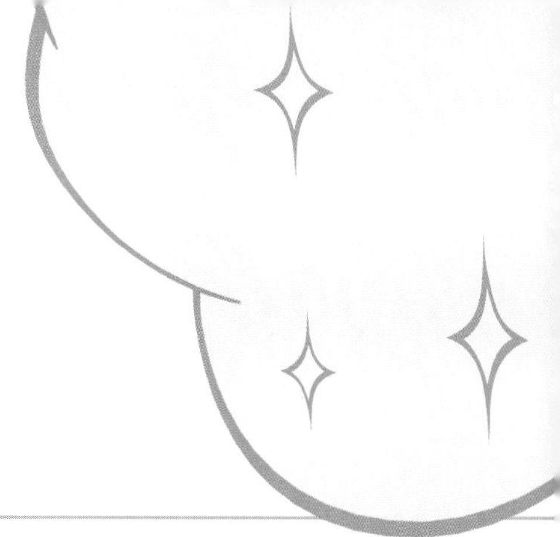

1. Follow the arrows to write the letter.

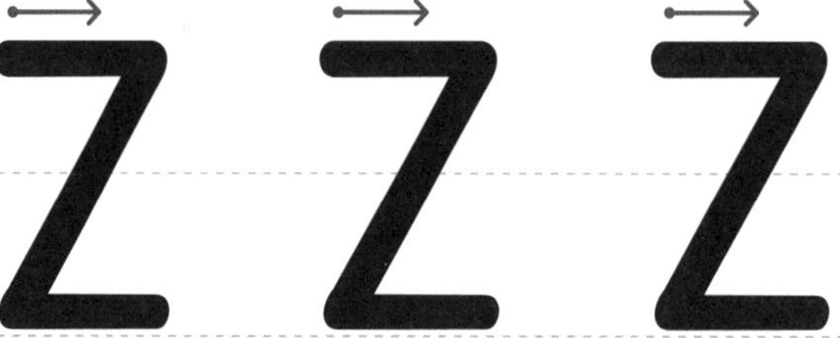

2. Trace the letter.

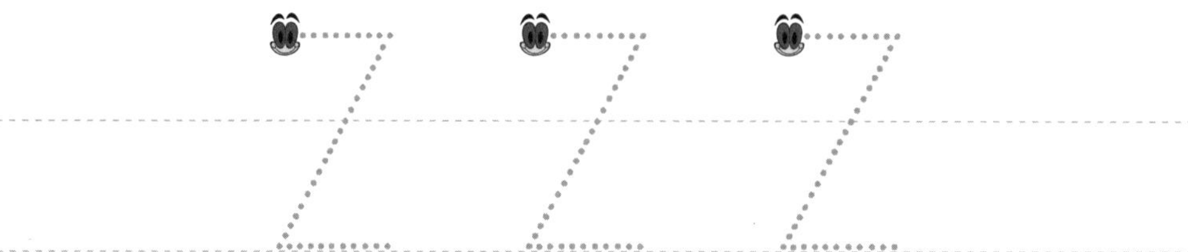

3. Now try writing it! Start with Bogart's emoji.

z z z

Choose the ending to Bogart's life story

Will it be a

happy ending?

Go to page **122**

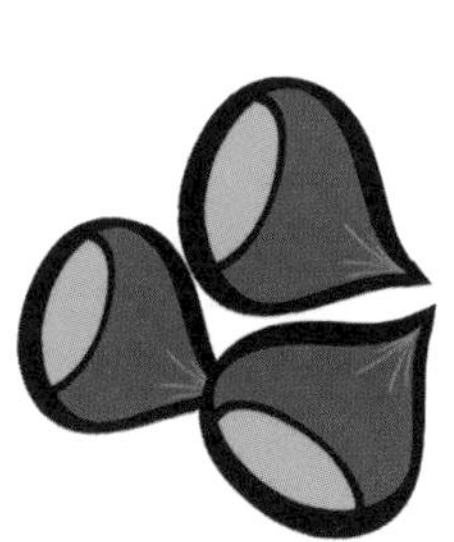

Will it be a

sad ending?

Go to page **126**

When Bogart woke up,
he felt very strange.

Could it be true?
Was he brand new?

Yes! Bogart had chomped his way out of Pooville!

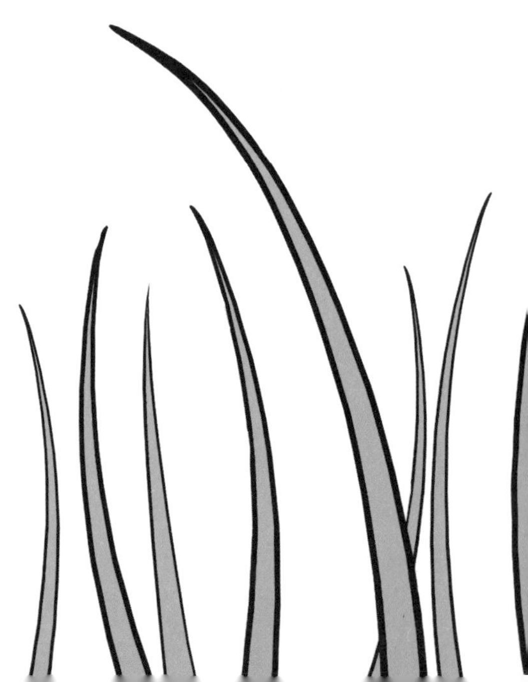

Anyone can
be a butterfly
if they try.

When Bogart woke up,
he felt very strange.

Could it be true?
Was he brand new?

Awww!
Keep chomping!

Let's Practise!

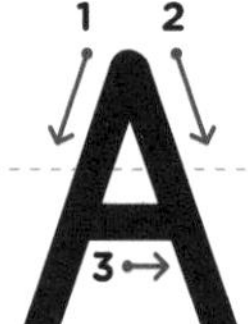

a

B

b

C

c

D

d

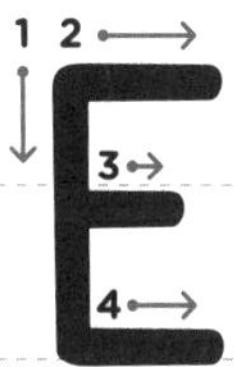

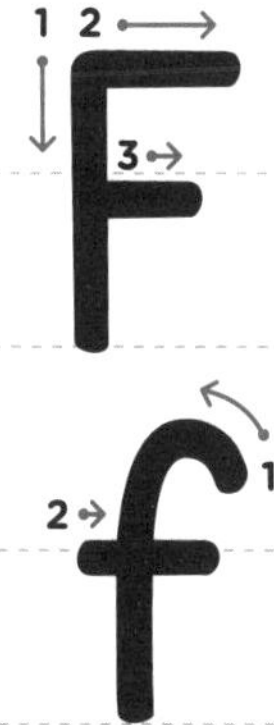

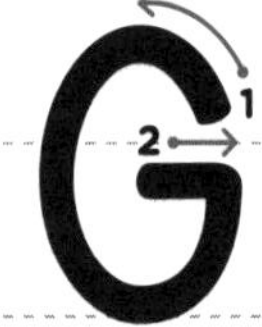
1
2

1
2

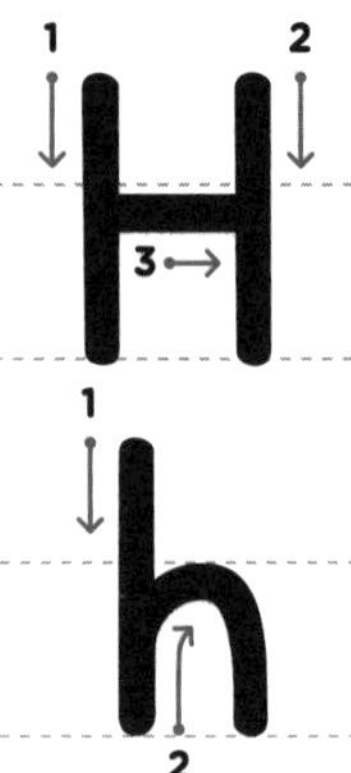
1
2
3
1
2

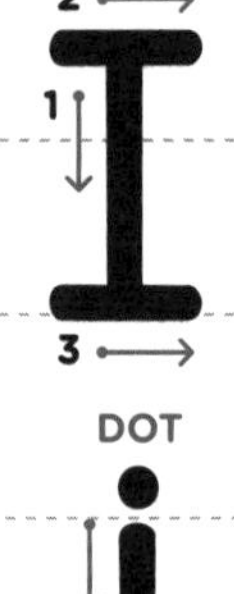
2
1
3
DOT

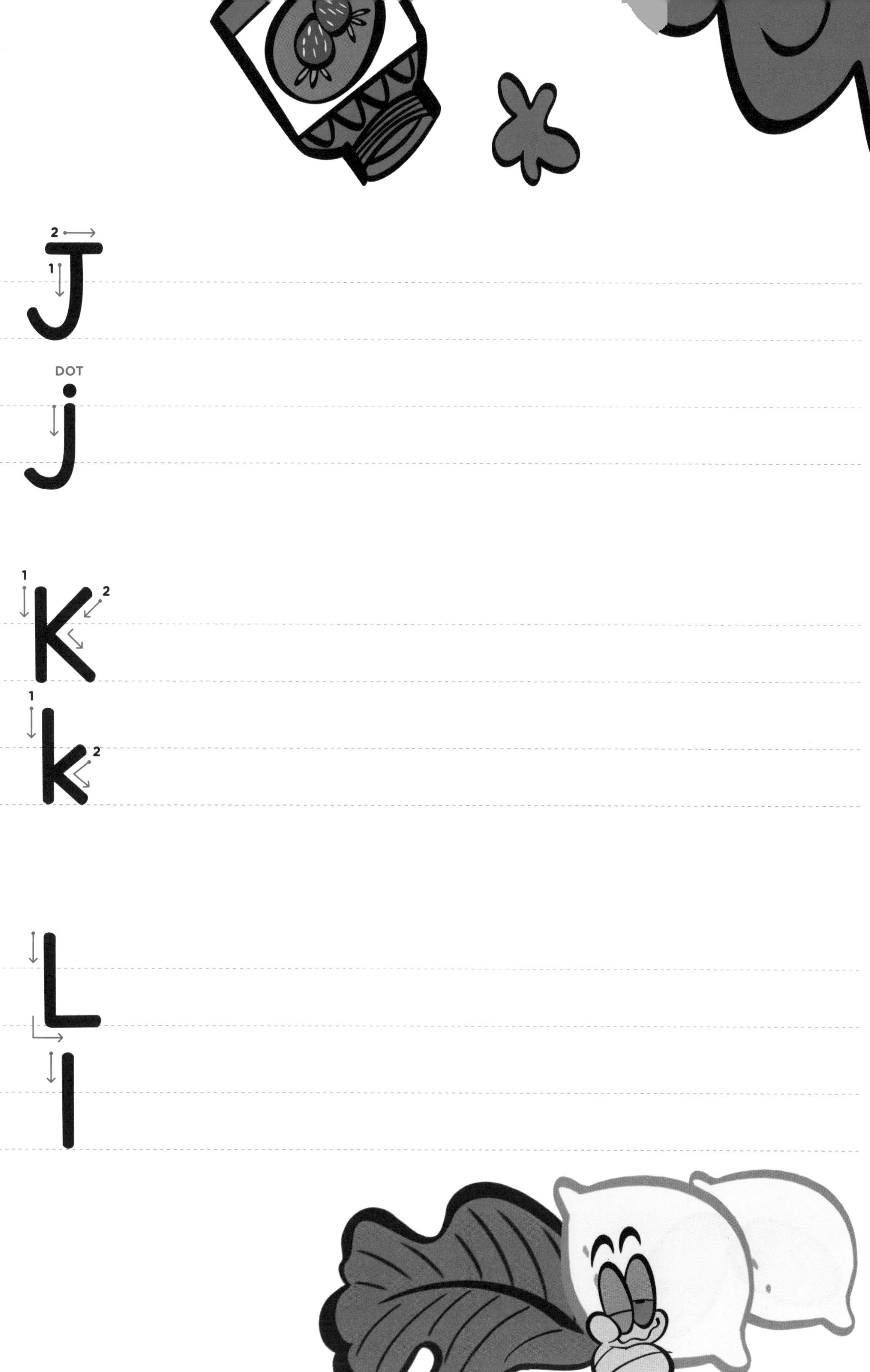
2
1
J
DOT
j
1
K
2
1
k
2
L
l

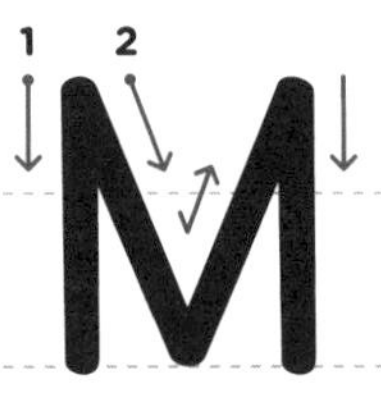

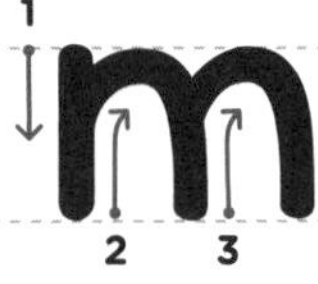

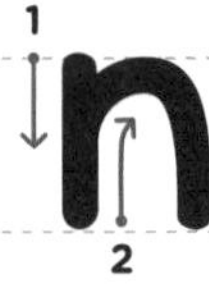

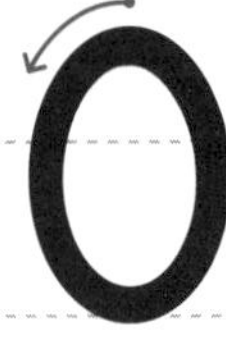

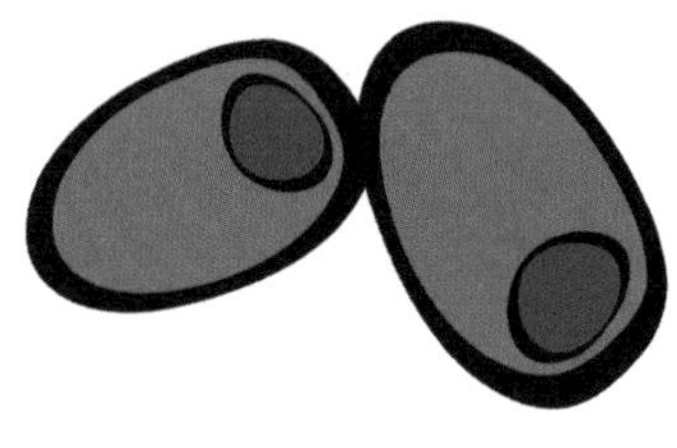

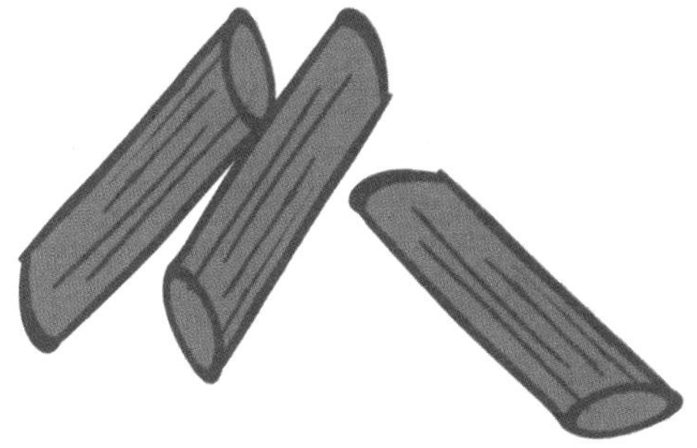

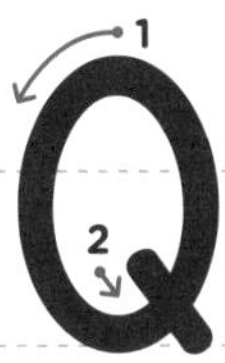

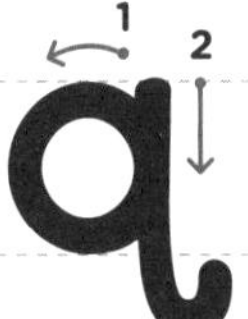

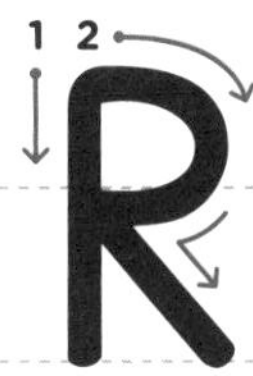

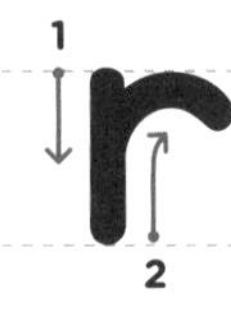

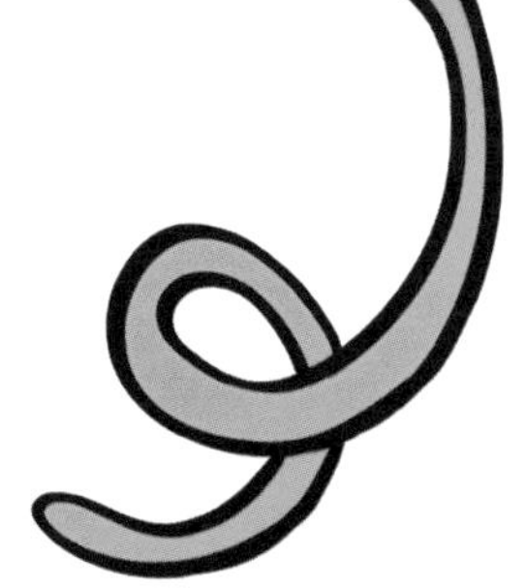

S

s

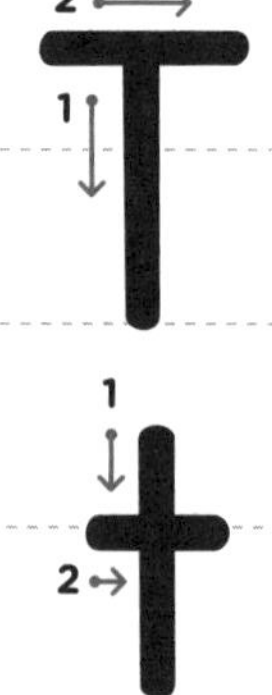

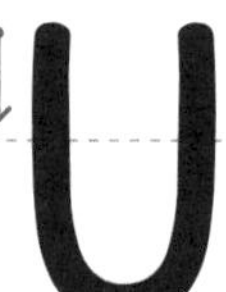

1 u 2

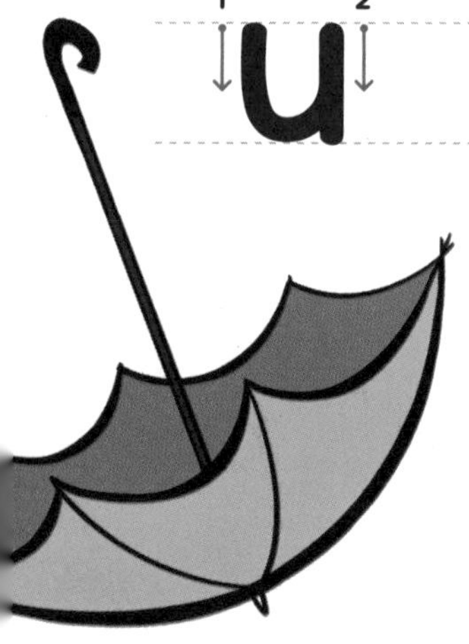

V

v

W

w

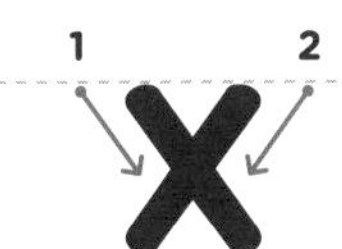

X

x

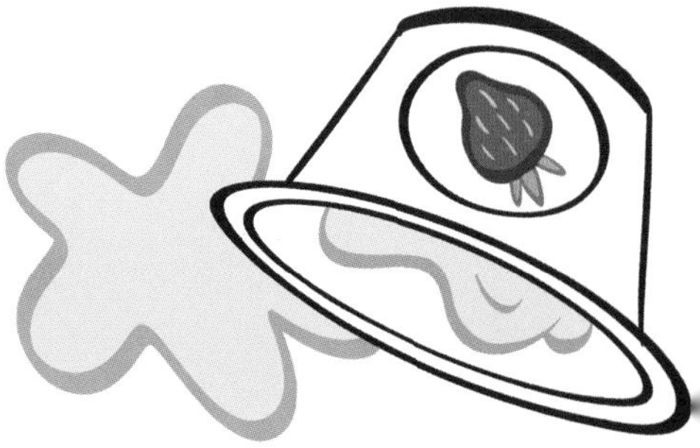

1 2
Y

1 2
y

Z

z

A to Z

Aa Bb Cc Dd Ee Ff Gg

Hh Ii Jj Kk Ll Mm Nn

Oo Pp Qq Rr Ss Tt Uu

Vv Ww Xx Yy Zz

MEET THE MRS WORDSMITH TEAM

Editor-in-Chief
Sofia Fenichell

Associate Creative Director
Lady San Pedro

Art Director
Craig Kellman

Writers
Tatiana Barnes
Mark Holland
Sawyer Eaton
Amelia Mehra

Researcher
Eleni Savva

Lexicographer
Ian Brookes

Designers
Suzanne Bullat
James Sales
Fabrice Gourdel
James Webb
Holly Jones
Caroline Henriksen
Jess Macadam

Producers
Eva Schumacher Payne
Leon Welters

Academic Advisors
Emma Madden
Prof. Susan Neuman

Project Managers
Senior Editor Helen Murray
Design Manager Sunita Gahir

Senior Production Editor Jennifer Murray
Senior Production Controller Louise Minihane
Publishing Director Mark Searle

DK Delhi
DTP Designers Satish Gaur and Rohit Rojal
Senior DTP Designer Pushpak Tyagi
Pre-production Manager Sunil Sharma
Managing Art Editor Romi Chakraborty

DK would like to thank Julia March for proofreading.

First published in Great Britain in 2021 by
Dorling Kindersley Limited
A Penguin Random House Company
DK, One Embassy Gardens, 8 Viaduct Gardens,
London, SW11 7BW

The authorised representative in the EEA is
Dorling Kindersley Verlag GmbH. Arnulfstr. 124,
80636 Munich, Germany.

This content is also available to purchase as *I Can Be a Butterfly*, a printable story and workbook at mrswordsmith.com

10 9 8 7 6 5 4 3
006–325949–August/2021

A CIP catalogue record for this book is available from the British Library.
ISBN 978-0-24152-713-9

Printed and bound in Malaysia

For the curious

www.dk.com

mrswordsmith.com

This book was made with Forest Stewardship Council™ certified paper – one small step in DK's commitment to a sustainable future.

GUIDE FOR GROWN-UPS

WRITE TO REMEMBER

Handwriting is a crucial skill for children as they move through their early school years, beginning with individual capital letters in Nursery (UK) or Pre-K (US) all the way to writing full sentences in Year 2 (UK) or 2nd Grade (US).

Handwriting helps consolidate children's knowledge of letters. Children (and adults) are more likely to retain new information by writing it down.

Write to remember is a simple rule of thumb. Research shows that children with better handwriting exhibit greater neural activation in brain regions associated with working memory and increased activation in the regions associated with reading and writing.

IT'S HOW YOU LEARN THE ALPHABET THAT MATTERS

Research shows that children with prior knowledge of the alphabet learn to read more easily and more fluently, so it's vitally important that the alphabet is taught in a playful and engaging way.

When learning their ABCs, children have to understand that each letter has a different shape and name, and that letters combine to form words.

By making it clear that the letter **A** is not just for **apple** but also for **avocado**, children learn that **A** makes a constant sound across different words, all linked by a familiar theme: food. Learning the most common sound that each letter makes is an essential, foundational skill that will be built on later when children encounter phonics.

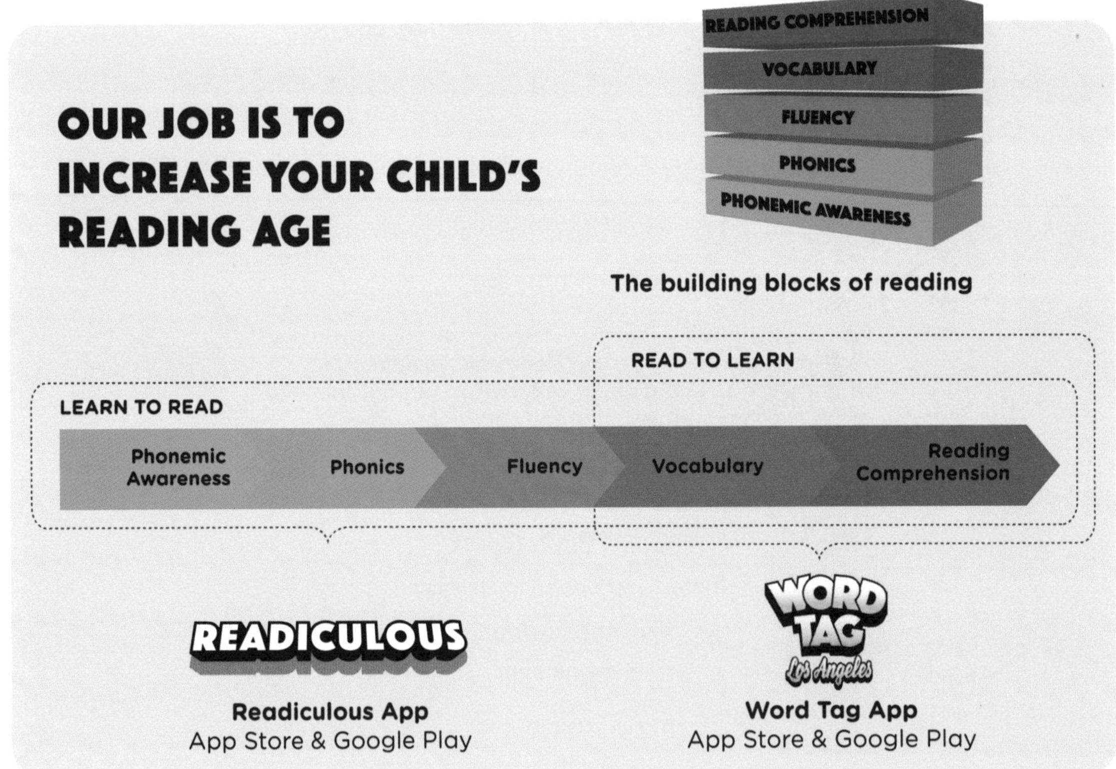

This book adheres to the science of reading. Our research-backed learning helps children progress through phonemic awareness, phonics, fluency, vocabulary, and reading comprehension.